What others are saying about
Be the Change: Acting with Intention
by Duanita G. Eleniak, PhD

A must read for everyone in the arts. The book follows the author's journey from the scientific to the sublime through her enrolment in a 9 month fine arts program studying acting for film and television while continuing her clinical therapy practice. It reads like a Hollywood film script complete with a cast of characters, plot twists and unusual phenomenon. One can't help but be inspired by this very courageous personal story of transformation from old patterns and old ways of being to enlightenment through the power of intention. Her story will help artists realize how their work can and does inspire higher levels of consciousness not only in themselves but in everyone who experiences their art. **G. Jaeger, Architecture Student, AIBC Assoc. RAIC Student member**

Duanita Eleniak's immersion in the performing arts takes us on a personal journey of transformation. Eleniak writes with a transparency and a vulnerability that touches our hearts and inspires a deeper relationship with spirit. A compelling read for those interested in transformation and the raising of consciousness!—**Dawn Sather, BSW RSW**

I am anchoring the rich tapestry of insight, lessons learned and wisdom the author has so courageously and generously shared. Her writing is quite sophisticated which revealed the quality of thoughts. In my books she has "joined the army of great minds" who have pioneered a new way of thinking and being via written words. Her angle (the arts) carves yet another precious face to the new thinking so called "new age" (NOT . . .) diamond. Kudos to her!—**Lorraine Jasmin**

I like the way the author is prepared to be surprised and entertained by the presence of Spirit in her life. Indeed, her faith is limitless and her writing style friendly and chatty, making it easy to engage the reader. The style is friendly, conveying a sense of awe and wonder with humour at the unfolding journey the author is having with Spirit in her life. Well done!—**Judith**

Dr. Duanita writes about communicating with Spirit with such ease, openness, honesty and refreshing humility. As she relates her experiences, I am so impressed at how eloquently she expresses in words the feelings and beliefs I have come to know throughout my life. I find myself eagerly reading on and I am at once amazed at her stories and feel like they are my stories too. I applaud her courage and incredible talent for writing so well on such a complex subject. I feel comforted and deeply grateful that there is someone in the world who believes what I believe. Dr. Duanita's passion and energy for communicating with Spirit has touched my heart and in my humble opinion, there is no better author on this topic.—**Kathryn**

Duanita's book gave me two really important lessons: the courage to be imperfect and the courage to put myself out there and brave what may come of it. I learned that in putting energy into the things that I really want out of life, I co-create what I want my future to be. She is one of those individuals that when you meet or have contact with her, she changes your life eternally for the better. Her book is but a piece of this energy force and reading it encouraged me to be a better person in both my personal and professional life. Thank you Duanita!—**Chasidy**

Reading Duanita's book allowed me to revisit an artistic part of myself that I had lost, and I am now on the journey to finding my creative self again. My experience with this book has catalyzed a number of events that assure me I am on the right path. Thank you!—**Catherine**

Duanita has given me the strength to believe in myself and to create for myself whatever I choose. Through my work with Duanita and her book I have experienced opportunities that I otherwise would have turned away from. Her book truly represents one of life's most important lessons—what you focus on expands. Thank you Duanita for being one of the most influential and positive people in my life!—**Cheryl**

Dr. Duanita explores realms which have yet to be explored. She is inspirational, courageous and energetic. In her sharings, she gives permission to her readers to explore their own limitations and gifts. She is truly brilliant.—**Diane**

Change is always a difficult thing, no matter what kind, our world and ourselves are always changing, Be the Change: Acting with Intention can inspire one and give hope, hopefully for many; it has for one for sure.—**Brad**

I have read Duanita's book. I love how she took a chance and immersed her whole self into the acting school and her roles. I also can relate to being frustrated, scared and unsure when doing something different and out of "your comfort zone". I was so grateful to read about the synchronicities, the messages that she was given and how she trusted "Team Spirit" to guide her and help her through. It gave me inspiration to continue on my journey of personal and spiritual awareness and allow myself to go where the "Spirit" takes me. Thank you Duanita.—**Lori**

Thank you—definitely what the world needs right now—how very timely.—**Serena**

What an incredibly profound video, not to mention an inspirational Ch. 11 in your book. I found both very moving and motivating, not only on an intellectual level, but on a deep, spiritually psychic level as well. We are all connected and intricately bound to one another and every living substance on earth, and you illustrate this beautifully with grace through your inquisitive nature. Your search for meaning in Truth, Spirit, and things that cannot be explained except through Universal Laws, has touched me beyond the depths of my soul, creating a sense of security, contentment and profound peace—peace that we all long to feel, and inevitably seek out but rarely find. The way you conclude Chapter 11, however, planted the seed for me to not look out, but to look within, for that peace and connectedness I long for is within me. It is within all of us. Well done Duanita! Your message comes across with dignity, finesse and grace, and encourages those who do not know, to want to know, and for those who do know, to want to know more. Because of your kindness, passion and dedication in sharing your knowledge with us, I am a better person because of it, with more compassion and understanding than ever before. You have taught me the tremendous Power I have within me, and how I can use it to heal myself, those around me, and the World. My blessings and endless thanks to you always. God Bless you.—**Jasmine**

Ms. Eleniak's description of her life experiences, like "crumbs of cheese", provide a path, if not a map of transition/ transformation from our ego centered "little self" to functioning as an integral component of our "divine self". She identifies markers on this path of transformation, i.e. the importance of trusting coincidence, multiple signs & feelings. These are all signals of a management system operating in a manner that requires a new type of attention. The reward of this new attention or "partnering with spirit", as Duanita calls it, is "oneness & harmony with the universe". Thank you, Duanita for sharing your journey & inspiring so many others along your path!—**John**

I very much enjoyed the chapter I read of Dr. Duanita Eleniak's new book! I really liked the story where Duanita is at her first day as a student in a new class and all the other students are much younger . . . we can all relate to that! How do I fit in? What can I do to best contribute? Then we get to the wonderful surprise where she is actually the inspiration to the rest of the class! Life is full of these affirming surprises, if only we can recognise and learn from them. Thanks, Duanita for an inspiring book!—**Kevin**

I have known Duanita for a very long time and it does not surprise me that she has written this book and that others receive her message with an open heart—even when their minds might be closed. She has always had this gift. This work is another in her life journey of seeking and finding and more than anything else—sharing. Sharing with conviction and passion.—**Connie**

Engaging, authentic and you are always inspiring! I feel very blessed by my connection to you. You have contributed greatly to assimilating my faith into my work. I believe your book is very important for people to be able to see how much they can do, be and invite into their lives if they only submit. "I am the pencil" as Mother Teresa said.—**Angela**

I see from your writing that your connection with the Spirit has moved you from mere believing and trusting into the zone of knowingness. So I guess you need no big sign to know that you are meant to be inspired and to inspire others. And yes, Moms know useful old recipes: have Faith and family is more important than work.—**Branka**

I think this writing is very relevant and accessible to all people. I was fully engaged while reading, and feel like the idea of partnering with Spirit more in my life is something I am left with more ideas and know-how around! thanks,—**Anna**

Duanita Eleniak's Be the Change: Acting with Intention is an honest map of the journey towards understanding that by dedicating ourselves to our passions we dedicate ourselves to creating a healthy reality. Duanita explores subjects that have been forbidden by scientific materialism and forms deep relationships with the mysteries that create magic and meaning in our lives. I left this book vibrating with the call to action!—**Rebecca**

Duanita, Thank you for sharing the fruits of your journey with the rest of us in such an expressive way.—**Nadia**

Duanita's book is inspiring. Readers get to sense her presence as well as her essence when reading Be the Change: Acting with Intention. One senses her essence through her words, gentle humour, and compassion for others. In short, we get to meet the ontological Duanita when we read her inspirational book!—**Andrea**

Dr. Duanita is indeed an inspiration! She pursues knowledge and understanding of life's connections relentlessly. Dr. Duanita illustrates a curiosity that requires her to continually question the connections between self and spirit. A curiosity that demands a deeper understanding, an understanding that she can then share with the world. Dr. Duanita did not hesitate to put herself "out there" throughout this exploration and clearly has given 100% to her work.—**Jan**

Be the Change

Acting with Intention

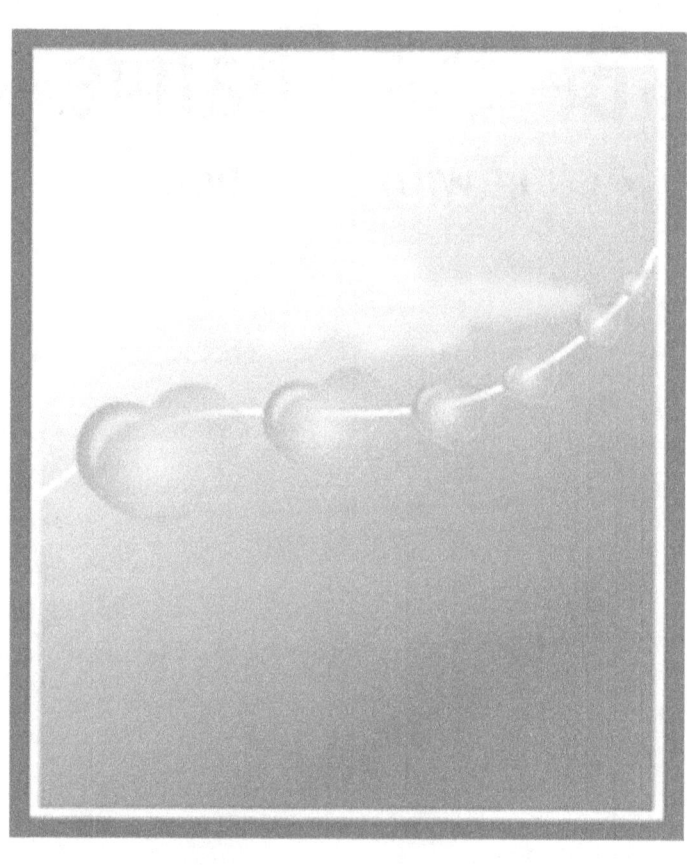

Be the Change
Acting with Intention

Duanita G. Eleniak, PhD

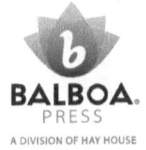

BALBOA.
PRESS
A DIVISION OF HAY HOUSE

Balboa Press books may be ordered through booksellers or by contacting:

Balboa Press
A Division of Hay House
1663 Liberty Drive
Bloomington, IN 47403
www.balboapress.com
1-(877) 407-4847

Because of the dynamic nature of the Internet, any web addresses or links contained in this book may have changed since publication and may no longer be valid. The views expressed in this work are solely those of the author and do not necessarily reflect the views of the publisher, and the publisher hereby disclaims any responsibility for them.

ISBN: 978-1-4525-4751-0 (sc)
ISBN: 978-1-4525-4750-3 (hc)
ISBN: 978-1-4525-4749-7 (e)

Library of Congress Control Number: 2012903321

The author of this book does not dispense medical advice or prescribe the use of any technique as a form of treatment for physical, emotional, or medical problems without the advice of a physician, either directly or indirectly. The intent of the author is only to offer information of a general nature to help you in your quest for emotional and spiritual well-being. In the event you use any of the information in this book for yourself, which is your constitutional right, the author and the publisher assume no responsibility for your actions.

Any people depicted in stock imagery provided by Thinkstock are models, and such images are being used for illustrative purposes only. Certain stock imagery © Thinkstock.

Printed in the United States of America

Balboa Press rev. date: 5/8/2012

Be the change you want to see in the world.
—Gandhi

Contents

Acknowledgements

This story only came to light with the help of many beings to whom I am deeply grateful.

First, to my daughter, Leila, and my family and friends, I send you a warm hug and thank you for all of your support and encouragement. Special thanks to Dr. Inula Martinkat and Jan Oberson for being my "mirrors." Immense gratitude to Lorie Cover, typist and psychic extraordinaire, who was my midwife for an earlier version of this story. Dr. Patricia Anderson, literary consultant, advised on publication. I am also very grateful to all of the authors and people who shared their ideas with the world so that I could have access.

To my publishing team Lisa Fuentes and Eileen Velthuis, I am forever grateful. I could not have done this without your help and lovely attention to details. Kathryn Lundy, Wise Web Woman, was the midwife for this book and helped to move it through to completion. Thank you.

Deep thanks to everyone at the New Image College of Fine Arts who gave me an experience that I will always treasure and to all of the people at the International University of Professional Studies who created a container that can accommodate explorations beyond the edges of reason.

And finally, thank you to Team Spirit who was with me every step of the way, guiding me and sending me messages that kept me motivated and inspired throughout this storytelling and beyond.

Introduction:
Agent of Inspiration

An all-encompassing worldview based in Spirit—this was the vision I carried with me before and during the writing of this book. Like so much of what guides my life, the vision came to me in a dream. I dreamt it during the time when I was thinking about how best to share the story of my recent personal journey of creativity and transformation. I had embarked on this journey with the aim of enhancing my own awareness and, at the same time, doing my best to awaken others to a spiritual worldview.

In the beginning, I was inclined to view myself as an agent of change. But as Gandhi advised, I also recognized that I must be the change that I want to see in the world. For, through my connection to Spirit, I am connected to all that is, and I thus affect all that is. Now, rather than an agent of change, I see myself as an agent of *inspiration*. And when I dreamt my vision, I knew without doubt that it came to me through Spirit.

I was so taken with the dream that I wanted it to be part of this world, too. With what now seems like a small miracle of communication, I managed to convey the essence of what I envisioned to a deaf artist, who rendered it as you see here:

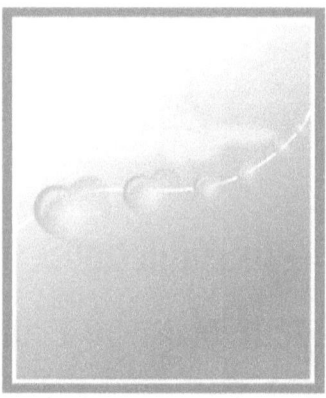

Air Love—a worldview envisioned
Designed by Siamak Ashrafinia

When he was done, the artist labelled the file "Air Love." And, indeed, I loved it! Together, the image and the words *Air Love* convey a vision of a worldview far beyond our current dominant paradigm, sometimes referred to as "scientific materialism." And the linked hearts suggest the oneness of us all—with each other, and with Spirit.

My experience as a clinical social worker, art therapist, philosopher, writer, and educator has convinced me that we are living in a unique time in history that offers unprecedented opportunities for each of us to grow in personal consciousness. I also believe that by seeking such growth we actively assist the realization of a worldview that incorporates Spirit and a deep respect for mystery.

With these ideas in mind, I set out on my journey of creative immersion, discovery, and, I dared to hope, expanding consciousness. I believed then, as I do now, that the arts and individual artistic expression are a powerful channel through which the collective consciousness of humankind can rise to a worldview of love, peace, joy, and truth. I began my journey with an exploration of the principles of the new science, in order to understand as much as I could about how shifts in consciousness happen. I then applied the concepts to myself as I immersed in a program of fine arts, studying acting for film and television. At the same time, I explored shifts in my own consciousness and also observed how the performing arts can transform others.

Although my story focuses on experiences with performance, readers engaged in all kinds of creative activities will see many commonalties linking their own endeavors and goals with mine. Throughout my program of artistic immersion, I actively engaged with Spirit, regularly using such tools and techniques as journaling, image making, affirmations, and more. Readers will be able to apply these in their lives to enhance individual creativity and motivation, as well as connection to Spirit.

As an individual, I have been, and remain, committed to assisting a shift in worldview. As an agent of inspiration, I challenge each of my readers to undertake the same commitment, by embracing Spirit, creativity, and transformation. Join me on an inspirational journey along the pathways of a worldview that, above all else, honors Spirit.

To take the first step, just turn this page . . .

one
Consciousness, Spirit, and the Arts

What Is Consciousness?

In a 1988 public television interview of the mythologist and author Joseph Campbell, Bill Moyers posed the question, "What is consciousness?" In response, Campbell spoke of the orchid growing up the tree by his lanai and described consciousness as the plant's "knowing" of where to grow and how to turn to the light.

Others, such as the psychiatrist Dr. David Hawkins, define consciousness as awareness—that part of us that takes in all of the subjective phenomena of life. In this awareness, I would discover, there is limitless potential.

The enlightened throughout history, authors of the modern physics, and other researchers have agreed that consciousness is both beyond form and, indeed, is the omnipotent matrix out of which form arises. Consciousness is the formless, invisible, infinite field of energy that is at once independent of time, space, or location yet is all-inclusive and ever present. In other words, through consciousness, potential moves from formless to form, from non-experienced to experienced. As Hawkins puts it, consciousness is a unified field "within which are variable levels of vibrational frequencies that appear as the observable universe."

One of the main difficulties of asking questions about consciousness is that the questions we raise, and therefore the answers we get, will be defined, and limited, by our own particular levels of consciousness. While this difficulty is unavoidable, it does not stop us from enlarging *our understanding* of the various levels, even though we might have yet to attain them. In 1995, Hawkins published a Map of Consciousness, the result of exhaustive investigation in which he applied research from the field of kinesiology to the study of consciousness. This map is a calibrated scale of the relative power of levels of awareness in all areas of human experience. It is a valuable tool that provides a way to measure changes in consciousness, or shifts in the vibrational frequency range.

Shifts in Consciousness

Hawkins's Map of Consciousness reveals that there are many levels of awareness available for humans to experience. The level of consciousness attained is aligned with each person's concept of self. The more limited the sense of self, the more constricted are the boundaries of experiencing, and the lower the calibration at that level of awareness. Rather than focusing solely on one's own consciousness, the goal, as Hawkins explains it, is to identify with consciousness itself and thus to know that one's actual self is *un*limited. This is the point at which we become "enlightened."

The characteristics of "pure" enlightened consciousness—as opposed to consciousness limited by our concepts of self—have been observed throughout human history. Such characteristics include a perception of timelessness, of being beyond form and time yet equally present everywhere. Enlightenment is a state where there is "oneness" with no recognition of separation—where, in place of ordinary thoughts and feelings, the individual often experiences a sense of infinite power, compassion, gentleness, and love. The historical literature of various spiritual disciplines reveals a variety of ways to shift and expand consciousness. The common denominator among these is an emphasis on eliminating the concept of self as a finite phenomenon.

Along with a rich repository of knowledge, practices, and techniques leading to pure consciousness, history has provided us with many blissful accounts of enlightenment—there is no doubt that shifts in consciousness can, and do, happen. Why, then, is the state of consciousness called enlightenment still relatively rare? The evidence is that, in modern society especially, few people take an active interest in becoming enlightened. If asked on the street, how many would claim such an achievement as their greatest ambition?

In the overall evolution of consciousness, only a very few people have chosen to commit to shifting their levels of consciousness in an expansive direction—even though it is possible. On average, a person advances little more than five points during a lifetime. In his 2005 book, *Truth vs. Falsehood*, Hawkins observed that human collective consciousness has also evolved very slowly:

> It did not reach level 90 until the time of the birth of the Buddha at approximately 563 B.C . . . by the time of the birth of Jesus Christ, the consciousness level of the totality of mankind had reached 100 . . . It took approximately 2000 years . . . to move from 100 to the level of 205 in the late 1980s.

The rise of human consciousness to a level above 200 is especially significant, because 200 marks the capacity to distinguish truth from falsehood. Level 200 is the threshold of empowerment, the beginning of a willingness to stop blaming and to accept responsibility for one's own actions, feelings, and beliefs. In other words, it was only in the late 1980s that collective consciousness reached a level associated with basic integrity, transitioning away from self-servingness to the more benign levels of caring for others. (See Hawkins' scale of consciousness in *Power versus Force*, 2002).

By November 2003, at the time of a spiritual event known as the Harmonic Concordance, the calibrated level of human consciousness had risen to an unprecedented 207. A factor in the relatively quick shift in collective awareness between the late 1980s and 2003 could have been the scientific community's increased interest in the study of consciousness—an interest that led to the new concept of a "science of wholeness," which captured the attention of physicists, astronomers, mathematicians, brain surgeons, and neurologists. The new science began to be mainstreamed into popular culture in the late 1980s, giving large numbers of people an expanded context and language in which to understand—and accept—knowledge about consciousness that was already well documented in spiritual literature. Before this, the slowness of humankind's shifts in consciousness may well have been due to a condition called paradigm blindness—an inability to see a particular reality until there develops a context and language for naming that reality.

The Consciousness of Worldviews

We are living in a unique time in history. The recent shift in humankind's general level of consciousness, the new science, and popular culture in the form of books, magazine articles, and films like *What the Bleep Do We Know!?* (2004) and *What the Bleep!?—Down the Rabbit Hole* (2006) have brought us to the brink of great change. Although a new worldview has yet to gain acceptance on a wide scale, people are now questioning the dominant paradigm or current worldview.

In a lecture delivered at the 2002 Prophets Conference in Florida, the late eminent psychiatrist Dr. John Mack defined "worldview" as what we see in "reality." It is what we think is so—how we structure reality. The purpose of a worldview is to provide us with a compass for living, a way to solve problems. The worldview, or paradigm, that any individual or collective might hold coincides with the level of consciousness attained by that individual or collective.

The current dominant Western worldview can be characterized as scientific materialism, the principal focus of which is on the material world. This perspective arose in the Middle Ages out of a sense of helplessness in the face of disease, war, and death; it was an attempt to understand and gain some control over the physical world and to learn its secrets. In the Middle Ages, this paradigm was still within a context of an ensouled world, but over the course of the last couple of centuries, science has arguably replaced soul or faith. The literal-mindedness of scientific materialism does not know what to do with the inner world, subjectivity, concepts of the Divine, ambiguity, paradox, uncertainty, and mystery. The distinguishing characteristic of this paradigm is reason, which emphasizes what is "logical" and "provable."

Inherent in this consciousness is a limitation at the calibrated level of 400. While this is the level of many great thinkers of history, such as Einstein and Freud, the problem with a worldview of reason is that its uppermost boundaries of consciousness end where the spiritual begins.

Reason, in other words, does not accommodate the entirety of truth and is thus a block to reaching higher levels of consciousness. Limited as we are by the perspective of scientific materialism, it is relatively uncommon for people in our society to transcend this level of consciousness.

There are, however, indications of the decline of scientific materialism as the dominant worldview. Many anomalies cannot always be explained with science—for example, crop circles, UFO abduction encounters, near-death experiences, and new data about consciousness. This suggests the need for a different way of knowing that would encompass our values, our connection to the Divine, our sense of the Sacred, the world of reflection, deep truths, and our spirit. Because scientific materialism has become a faith in and of itself, with no connection to the Divine, we have been left empty. To fill the void, more and more people have sought out experiences of "non-ordinary" states of consciousness—through, for example, the use of psychedelics, meditation, and holotropic breathwork. People's increasing openness to the Divine, and to mysticism as a legitimate way of knowing, is a major sign of transition to a new worldview with its corresponding shift in consciousness.

By the time of the 2002 Florida Prophets Conference, Dr. Mack had devoted his life to shifting the worldview of scientific materialism. He provided passionate reasons to do so, and his words went to the heart of some of our most deeply felt contemporary concerns. When we live only in and for material reality, we only enjoy what we can take from that reality, and "the world becomes little more than real estate." From a consciousness so limited come "wars, environmental desecration, and animals being treated as 'products' rather than entities/spirits." Technology, Mack added, was not the solution but part of the problem: "As we slip into 'technological autism' we can no longer hear the cries of the animals or see the misery of human beings. It is this obvious destructiveness that points to the need for a profound shift in worldview."

But how exactly does this shift begin? Mack and other researchers agree that what must happen is a change in our attitude of mind—to an understanding that takes us beyond the physical world, enabling us to accept that consciousness is real. Such a shift in worldview would respect mystery; the Eternal; the Cosmos of Abundance; and the oneness of physical, metaphoric, and mythic reality. It would open up a new world of possibilities—among them that an inherent intelligence is at work in our Universe, and that there may be universes with different physical laws. As Mack expressed it, a shift in worldview "changes the sense of who we are, of what it means to be a human being. There is more of a sense of connectedness with everything, the joyous and the painful . . . We become the instruments of creation unfolding . . . which is joyous and also awesome."

In terms of Hawkins' Map of Consciousness, such a shift in paradigm would calibrate at energy levels of 500 and over, exactly the point at which awareness expands not just in power but in quality. Inherent at these levels of consciousness are love, joy, peace, and enlightenment. At the levels where consciousness vibrates at a higher frequency than reason, love is the great motivator. The corresponding worldview would encompass and nurture altruism, compassion, dedication to principles, inspirational leadership, and creative expression. Above all, the new worldview would incorporate Spirit and an understanding of the consciousness of the Universe.

Understanding the Consciousness of the Universe

The critical advances in scientific knowledge that occurred late in the 20th century have provided a necessary bridge from science to the wisdom of religion and philosophy; thus we now have an enhanced possibility of shifting to a new dominant worldview and a level of consciousness that would include Spirit. In 1975 Fritjof Capra wrote a pioneering work, *The Tao of Physics*, in which he outlined the ways in which modern physics and Eastern mysticism are harmonious and consistent. Indeed, the basic elements of understanding the Universe—on which science, religion, and philosophy are now beginning to agree—are truths that have been known and written about in all major spiritual systems.

The first of these truths concerns the basic "oneness" of the Universe. That is, we are all one, interconnected and indivisible, and this includes connection between abstract and material realities. This view is also the central characteristic of the mystical experience, that is, of a direct, non-intellectual experience of reality. The idea of oneness also runs through several insights gained through quantum physics—and the implications are far-reaching. This understanding not only unites everything that happens in the visible outer world, but it also links the inner subjective world to the outer world.

The second basic truth about the Universe is that it is an intelligent field that is inherently conscious. It is through this field of energy that the inner and outer worlds are connected. In the arena of quantum physics, awareness of the energy field is rather new; it therefore goes by a number of names, including the Unity Field, the Matrix, the Quantum Hologram, Nature's Mind, the Mind of God, and, most often, the "field." In 1917 Dr. Max Planck, considered to be the father of quantum physics, first referred to this intelligent, unseen power of nature responsible for our physical world. Behind this force, he said, we must assume "the existence of a conscious and intelligent mind . . . the matrix of all matter." Now, decades later, many scientists have followed in the wake of Planck's thought, echoing in their own way what the spiritual masters have been saying for centuries. An essential "discovery" of the new science—important particularly to the idea that consciousness can shift—is that the field is constantly moving, flowing, and changing. It is thus a dynamic field of interrelated events, and the mutual interrelations determine the structure of the whole.

This leads to the third basic truth about the Universe, the idea that it is participatory. We are connected to this larger field of consciousness through our thoughts and feelings. Because of the unity of all, the observer participates in an event simply by observing and can no longer claim the position of detached, objective observer. The concept of "participation" instead of "observation" is also inherent in the tradition of mystical knowledge, which takes it even further, to a point where observer and observed are indistinguishable in their oneness. With the recognition that nothing is separate, that the subjective and the objective (the observer and the observed) are one and the same, it becomes possible to transcend a view of the world that emphasizes duality. To observe is to participate.

The fourth truth that we must therefore recognize is our own personal responsibility—that is, our most minute day-to-day choices of thoughts and feelings, as well as our behaviors, impact the field in which we live and everything that is within it. We have enormous power for change and creation, and with this power comes our responsibility as human beings to attend to our personal level of consciousness and the quality of our connection to the Universe. Research indicates that the field contains an infinite number of potential realities existing simultaneously as waves of possibility. When an individual consciousness focuses, the wave becomes the particle, or the reality, experienced. This might also be described as a mirror effect: our thoughts, feelings, emotions, and beliefs—indeed, our level of consciousness—are reflected in the world around us through the field, which reflects without bias or judgment. This latter point is very important because it implies that the reality co-created by an observer and the field is dependent upon the observer's level of consciousness.

A growing number of researchers are finding evidence of the substantial role that thoughts and feelings play in co-creating reality. Noteworthy among them is Dr. Candace Pert, whose pioneering research established the biomolecular basis for our emotions, providing empirical evidence for the mind-body link. Such research verifies the role that emotions and feelings play in bridging the inner subjective world of emotion to the "real" world of matter, in this case, the outer forms of our bodies. In documenting the power of our thoughts and emotions to create our realities, the scientific language and evidence might be new, but the concept is not. Mystics, Eastern philosophers, shamans, rishis, and alternative practitioners and teachers have long been connecting to the field through thoughts and feeling states, using such methods as affirmations, intentions, and prayers.

Now that such practices can be articulated in the language of science, ever greater numbers of people acknowledge that we co-create the realities of our life and the world.

The promise of this new knowledge is awe inspiring. We now know that not only do our overt actions and behaviors impact the world, but so, too, do every one of our thoughts and feelings. We can take responsibility for our thoughts and feelings, and we can change them. We can shift our consciousness and, in doing so, attract different realities into our life and the world.

We know that if we change ourselves and/or our reality, we impact the entirety of the whole to which we are connected in the field. We are conscious beings in a conscious Universe, creating the world through our observations and our level of awareness. As we more fully understand how this works, we assume more responsibility for creating the reality in which we live, including the dominant worldview. Since the field, like a mirror, reflects back thoughts and feelings in a literal way, the onus is on us. The power we have as human beings to co-create reality can either be exercised in an expansive, high-vibrational way, embracing values like love, peace, and joy; or it can be used in a constrictive, low-vibrational way, embracing values like hate, anger, grief, and violence. As we become more aware of our consciousness and the role it plays in creation, increasingly we are called to choose.

Each of us can direct our thoughts and feelings and thereby choose what level of consciousness we wish to create—for ourselves and in the world. This implies the need for a strong ethical base and strong self-esteem if choices are to lead to a more spiritual world view. On a mass scale, we need to evoke *feelings* that vibrate at level 500 or higher, the level just past the levels of reason. If a critical mass of people began feeling such high-energy emotions, this would quickly attract a worldview of the kind I envisioned in my dream of Air Love—a worldview of joy, peace, enlightenment, oneness, and Spirit. The question is: How do you create a situation that would allow the greatest number of people to experience high levels of consciousness or, at the very least, to begin to *feel* their way into these levels?

The Role of the Arts

There are many ways that people might suddenly awaken to a more expansive view of reality—UFO encounters, near-death experiences, out-of-body experiences, epiphanies, guru contacts, and lucid dreams, to name a few. The unpredictability with which such experiences occur, however, rules them out as reliable methods for assisting a quick shift in collective consciousness. Such experiences are also not necessarily within the control of a majority of the population and are not a productive way of reaching the greatest number of people possible.

Education has afforded another avenue through which to shift the worldview. Conferences, lectures, and books abound, carrying information on a more expansive view of the Universe. *What the Bleep Do We Know!?* (2004), *What the Bleep!?—Down the Rabbit Hole* (2006), and *The Secret* (2006) are examples of recent movies promoting a paradigm shift; they have gained popularity among a widespread audience. These attempts to inform people of the new reality are commendable, but they are only a first step. And by their very nature, as reasoned educational endeavors, they are self-limited at the threshold just before the leap to vibrations above 500. A worldview built on a paradigm vibrating above the level of reason must include what Don Juan called "silent knowledge." It must be able to be conveyed through ways other than written and spoken words, because Spirit would be an inherent factor in the new worldview. And Spirit, or the field, is by nature beyond not only words but also beyond boundaries, symbols, and form itself.

The creative arts offer something more than educational programs, tools, and curricula. The arts elicit feelings and take us into dimensions beyond reason. Traditionally, the arts have also been a secular expression of humankind's highest spiritual aspirations. They open a path that we can consciously and intentionally choose to enter. Through direct emotional and spiritual appeal to the audience, the arts have the capacity to move and shift people's consciousness—to be the "knock" that opens people to an awareness of a greater reality.

Unlike some of the other ways to shift consciousness, the fine arts are widely accessible and are a daily part of many people's lives. They reach masses of people every day through music, television, movies, architecture, plays, and images. Yet, as familiar in our lives as they are, the arts offer more than just basic fare. In support of a shift to a spiritual worldview, the arts impart vision. Because the fine arts vibrate at high levels, they have the ability to evoke states of consciousness outside of time in a place where vision is possible. They also have the inherent ability to invite an audience on a journey to see what a spiritual worldview would be like. Such vision is crucial, for it is in being able to imagine things from the end, from the place where you want it to be, that you can more easily access the feelings of that place and more quickly manifest the desired reality.

In the course of my research into the arts I made a final, highly significant discovery. The arts, I learned, possess qualities that some authors have described as characteristic of the field, or Spirit, or God Mind. Foremost among these qualities is creativity. In his 2004 book, *The Power of Intention*, Dr. Wayne Dyer (2004) asserts that the field, or Spirit, is essentially and inherently creative. If it were not, "nothing would come into existence." Julia Cameron supports this statement in her book *The Artist's Way: A Spiritual Path to Creativity* (1992), in which she states that spirituality and creativity are one and the same force. In her work with artists, she found that connection with the creative force entailed acknowledging a larger Spirit.

By the time I reached this point in my exploration of the arts, I was convinced that the arts, and those who create them, play a major role in guiding the imagination and vision of a society. The more I delved into the web of connections among creative endeavor, human feelings, and spirituality, the more I could also see that the arts open a way through which the shift to a more spiritual worldview can happen quickly and effectively—offering the hope of transforming a world on the brink of destruction.

A Question of Choice

Through my research into the new physics and the arts, my personal goals were now clear. I had an intense desire to be as powerful an instrument of change in the world as I could possibly manage. I was committed to assisting the forces of the Universe to give birth to a fully conscious and working worldview based in spirituality. I wanted to effect changes in humanity on a much larger scale than just the people in my private practice. I also realized the need to make such shifts quickly if we were, as a world, to move to a more spiritual creation of reality.

Because of my interest in the arts, I was inspired by Barbara Marx-Hubbard's plea to artists at the 2002 Prophets Conference in Florida. In her address to the audience, this author and futurist made a call for artists to support the current movement into what she termed "the age of conscious evolution through co-creation"—to dramatize the transcendent capacities of human beings and bring these to life. This, I decided, was what I wanted to attempt—to go beyond the written word about what transcendence is and how we get there and, instead, to actually do it. I would take the principles of co-creating reality that I had researched and make myself the subject of a consciousness-transforming experiment. While always operating at, or above, the level of integrity, I would use artistic expression to assist as many people as possible to a level of consciousness beyond reason—by showing them a vision of the new, more spiritually based worldview.

There was no doubt in my mind that the time was right for my undertaking. Today's visionaries, scientists, and prophets in the arena of consciousness all agree that we are living at an extraordinary time in the evolution of human awareness and the opening of a wider worldview. In these early years of the 21st century, new discoveries in science have shifted perceptions of our relationship to nature and given it new meaning. We are at a point in history when we can all be creators of our future and—to guide our choices—imagination, participation, and responsibility are crucial. Artists must stand with scientists, researchers, and religious leaders to portray truth in a way that can awaken people to a vision of peace, integrity, harmony, love, and joy. In today's world, artists are essential as ambassadors of the Creative Energy that underlies our new under-standing of reality.

As I thought about the role of the arts in the transformation of consciousness, one question was foremost in my mind. To fulfill my purpose of assisting the expansion in worldview by eliciting spiritually based feelings from a large number of people, I needed to set off on the right path. Which area of the arts, I wondered, would offer me the most promising direction for my journey?

My continuing investigation of the new science and the arts, alongside the insights of other researchers, gave me the answer I sought. I decided that the performance arts would best further my goals. Film and television and, to a lesser degree, stage are enormously popular; they can attract an audience of the greatest number of people. Forms like paintings, sculpture, photography, and music can be incorporated into film and/or television, which in turn can be adapted for Internet use—again drawing a wide audience. Finally, since a worldview based on spirituality goes past reason and into a realm beyond words, the images, colors, and sound of film and television make them ideal media to communicate a new vision of reality.

I knew what I had to do.

I enrolled in a nine-month fine arts immersion program, specializing in acting for film and television. I vowed to approach the program as a way of becoming more aware of my personal power. I would make small daily choices to change my consciousness in the consistent direction of expanding integrity and increased alignment with Spirit. I hoped that, through my example and performances, others might also move in this direction. If this can happen, I believed, then collective awareness can rise—potentially lifting up everyone and everything in our collective ocean of consciousness. With such hope and faith, I embarked on what would become a life-changing journey of transformation.

two

"Team Spirit" and First Steps

The Journey Begins

When I first set out on my journey of transformation, I was 45 years old, 5'4", and 120 pounds, with blue eyes, strawberry blond hair (when colored—gray when not). I came from a middle-class back-ground and was university educated with a Masters in Social Work (dual concentration in both clinical practice and research), a Masters diploma in Art Therapy and a "just about" Masters degree in Theology. I was also divorced, single, and living with my 11-year-old daughter and two dogs, a golden retriever and Jack Russell, in a small coastal suburb in North Vancouver, Canada. Of Ukrainian heritage, I was raised in the Catholic faith. I was not practicing Catholicism in a formal way but was still incorporating faith into my daily life.

I took stock of myself in this way on account of the principle of oneness. I knew that even the most minute detail of myself and my life would be inseparable from the journey and its outcome. I felt that this would be true in ways that I might not see or predict in the moment, but which would become clearer as my consciousness transformed.

My unknowing "traveling companions" at this time were people at the fine arts college where I had enrolled in the immersion program in film and television acting. They included 11 fellow students—8 women and 3 men. The majority of the students ranged in age from 18 to 20 years old; one male student was in his early 30s and one in his late 20s. There were

11 teachers (10 men and 1 woman), ranging in age from early 30s to early 60s. The people at the college were aware that I was doing the program as part of my PhD research. But I offered no further details and no one questioned me.

At my side throughout was "Team Spirit." This was the name I gave to the energy of the Universe, or the consciousness of the field, and which I actively invited to accompany me on my journey. Spirit, or universal energy, would be with me every step of the way. I believed that this energy had a consciousness independent of, yet still connected with, me. I regarded the energy as loving, kind, abundant, positive, and able to reflect back reality to me like a mirror.

Morning Pages

To inspire me along the path I had chosen, and to enhance my connection with Team Spirit, I used a number of tools and techniques. Among the most important were Morning Pages, a tool for breaking through creative blocks. Julia Cameron, who developed the concept of Morning Pages, describes them and their use in her 1992 book *The Artist's Way: A Spiritual Path to Creativity*. Before, during, and after my nine-month immersion in the fine arts program, I wrote at least three pages, longhand, every morning. At the end of this book, **Creative Inspiration** I give a few excerpts from my Morning Pages, and I share more of such writings as my journey unfolds in coming chapters.

I worked with the Morning Pages in many ways. For example, I used them to apply the principles I was learning about how to bring forth new realities to the creative projects in which I was involved at the time. The theory says that realities exist simultaneously and that the reality that pops into being results from our placing attention on it and choosing it. What attracts a particular reality is the vibrational quality of what a particular reality *feels* like—it is the *feeling* that draws to us the reality. So, in my Morning Pages, I would write about my "realities" "as if" they were already happening in the way that I intended them to. This allowed me to develop a vision of my intentions and elicit feelings of what the reality would be like. I would find myself altering the way I felt as I sunk into my affirmative writing of a situation as I imagined it. I would explore possibilities and options on the page, discovering what different realities "felt" like. I then was able to choose what felt best for me.

I considered it crucially important to treat the Morning Pages as a journal of communication with Team Spirit—the mysterious force that runs through all Creation. In my Morning Pages I refer to this energy formally, using many different salutations. Sometimes I would use the vocabulary from my childhood as a Ukrainian Catholic, saying, for example, "God." This, however, is a term I tend to avoid because, over the years, it has become controversial and can trigger many associations for people. As I more fully realized how essential this force was to my creative endeavors, I began to use the term "Team Spirit," recognizing that the force helping me had many elements to it. I also called upon many energies to assist me (angels, saints, Beings of Christ Consciousness), and I noted these by name in my writings.

Supported by the constant presence of Team Spirit, I used the Morning Pages to gather together various techniques to help me actively fulfill my goals. In this way, the Morning Pages became a reflective journal in which I recorded dilemmas and decisions throughout my creative projects.

I would begin a typical morning's entry using the "Co-create Your Day" format proposed by Dr. Joe Dispenza in the movie *What the Bleep Do We Know!?* This included a formal invocation of Team Spirit and the consciousness of the Universe to be present with me throughout my day, a stated intention for the day, and a request for communication from Team Spirit in the form of signs or synchronicities. I would then record all my dreams from the previous evening. Dreams have long been known as a way through which the universal energies communicate to humans, and I paid attention to all my dreams. In fact, at the time I had been doing dream work formally for 20 years.

Additionally, I would always include a section of positive affirmations in my Morning Pages. Research indicates the effectiveness of affirmations in bringing realities into existence. I would alternately create my own affirmations, find affirmations I liked and work with them, and/or adapt affirmations from whatever reading material inspired me at the time. My "work" with affirmations included writing them out repetitively from 3 to 10 times each on a daily basis. I made a point of cultivating an "attitude of gratitude" by writing a paragraph of affirmations of everything I was grateful for at the time. The expression of gratitude is strongly linked to the reality of abundance and can be one of the most effective affirmations.

I would also write prayers in the Morning Pages. The formal prayer that I most consistently wrote on a daily basis was "An Artist's Prayer," by Julia Cameron. I made some alterations to the original, however, in order to change all the words to a positive focus in the present. To the end of the prayer, for instance, I added the reassurance that the world is as it should be:

Help us to know that we are never alone,
that we are loved and lovable.

Help us to create as an act of worship to you.

All is well in the world.

Other Tools and Techniques

At the beginning of, and indeed throughout, my journey of creativity and transformation, I found subliminal tapes to be very helpful. The main one I used was Louise Hay's *Subliminal Tape on Self-Esteem* (1998). On one side of the tape are verbal positive affirmations about self. On the other, one hears only music, while the affirmations are repeated using subliminal technology in order to bypass any negative critic one might have at a conscious level that could stop positive statements about self from being integrated at deep levels. The positive statements are sent through subliminal processes to layers of the subconscious or unconscious mind.

The tape came with instructions to listen to it once a day for 30 days. But I actually began by listening to it once a day for two 40—day periods. After that, I would listen to the tape whenever I was faced with doing something that was particularly challenging for me. Initially, I listened to the side of the tape with verbal positive affirmations only a couple of times, because I found myself reacting negatively to the content—that is, telling myself that certain positive affirmations were untrue for me. After the first three months of listening only to the music side of the tape, I was easily able to affirm the positive statements of self and, therefore, would listen to both sides of the tapes.

I made this effort to consciously enhance my self-esteem because of the crucial role that personal choice has in the process of shifting awareness. Ensuring that I made the best possible choices necessarily required me to have strong self-esteem. Because of the success I experienced with Louise Hay's tape, I experimented with other subliminal tapes. In the end, I avoided any whose wording was framed in a "what you don't want" rather than in a "what you want" way. My advice for others is to be similarly wary of tapes with negative wording, however well meaning. Such inattention to the impact of words, I believe, puts the listener at risk of implanting and affirming realities that would be better avoided.

In addition to subliminal tapes, I also used visual imagery to support my intentions, to help actualize the new reality I sought, and to enhance my positive affirmations. Bearing in mind that shifting consciousness beyond the level of reason often requires ways other than words, I was drawn to image making. Images are one of the natural languages of the unconscious realms, as shown by our dreams. Many people have recognized and successfully used images as powerful tools in the manifestation or creation process. Think of Disney, for one. To communicate my artistic intentions as effectively as possible, I therefore not only wrote them down but also created them in collage images.

For example, as a beginning actress, I decided to intentionally create an image of the performer I planned on becoming. In my mind, and on paper, I collaged together an artist based on several people whom I admired. In my Morning Pages, I named them and described what they represented to me:

> Sophia Loren (because she is a woman who knows she is beautiful; because she still remained very "real" throughout her career); Shirley MacLaine (because she is a great dancer, a mystic that speaks out in the world, and she continues to act into her 70s); Julie Andrews (because of her phenomenal voice range and the fact that she continues to act into her 70s); Julia Cameron (because she has brilliant insight into the creative process and can teach this in a simple way; because she is a brilliant and prolific writer who continually takes risks); Faye Dunaway

(because of the advocacy role she has taken with regard to the amount and type of roles available for women over 50 in Hollywood); Audrey Hepburn (because of her passion for dance and incomparable style); and one of my teachers, Philip Granger (because of his inspiration to simply love what one is doing).

Here is the collage image that I created, and which would inspire me over and over as I immersed myself in the art of performance:

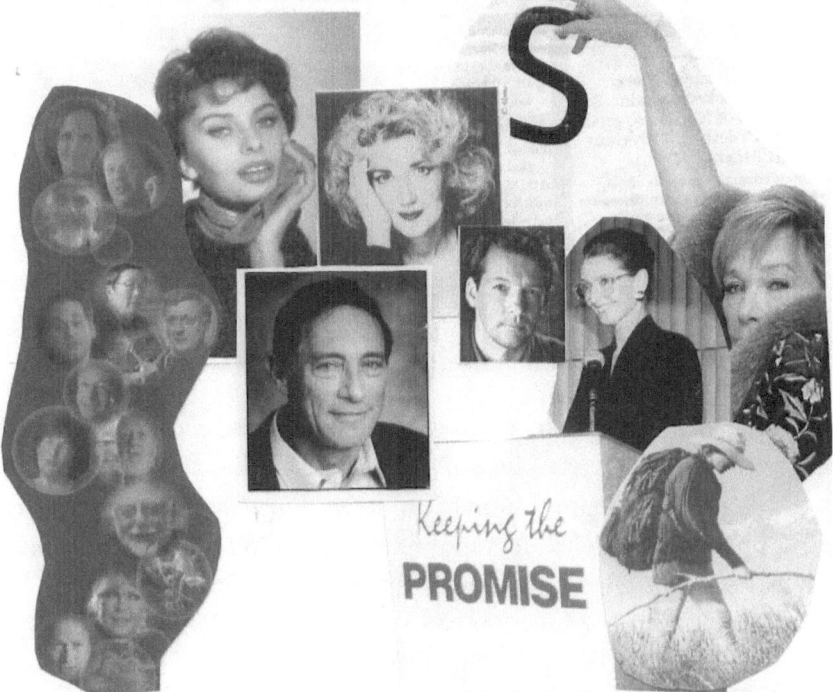

Here is an example of collage images I used when working on bringing into reality different parts of myself. I took images of people who inspire me with a quality that they have that I would like to develop. I then placed these images in picture frames in places that I would see so that I had continual reminders that the qualities that I was bringing into reality in myself were already with me...in reality...in the images of these people.

In addition to the images, I also wrote affirmations, for example: I am a brilliant and prolific writer (Julia Cameron) who can also appreciate her beauty (Sophia Lauren, Audrey Hepburn). I love to sing and dance and actually have talent for it (Audrey Hepburn, Shirley MacLean). I have brilliant ideas and really understand the theoretical information presented by the quantum physics material (images of all of the scientists in *What the Bleep Do We Know!?*). I am an actress who knows how to create reality in imaginary circumstances and who has mastered the use of atmosphere and character development (Philip Granger). I am committed to a life in service of assisting the shift in consciousness above the levels of integrity (Dr. John Mack).

Inspirational collage affirming my reality as a performing artist

I have long used collage making based on intentions in my private practice with clients who wish to change aspects of their life. Successful results similar to those that I have seen happen are documented in Julia Cameron's *The Artist's Way*. After making my own collage images, I put them in places where I would see them often and maintain my awareness of them: for example, framed by my bedside, on the wall, and in the front jacket of my school binder. For a glimpse of the power that collage making can have in one's life, see **Creative Inspiration II**, "Sharing Miracles" (written as Duanita Gaye, my pseudonym as an artist).

In addition to doing collage work, I had professional photographs of myself taken just before entering the arts immersion program. I would sit again for photographs midway through the immersion and at the end. These photographs are a visual record of shifts in consciousness as they materialized in my body:

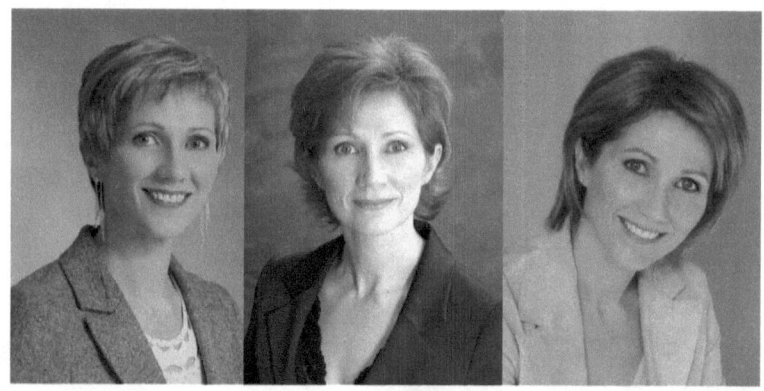

Left: before the beginning of the immersion, *photograph by Evangelos*; center: middle of the immersion, *photograph by Trevan Wong*; right: end of the immersion, *photograph by Douglas Buchan*

As I gained performance experience, I would also gather photo-graphs of some of the characters I became, including "Billie" from the play *Balm in Gilead* and "Ivy Pepper" from the film *Cleaning House*. By the end of my arts immersion, I also had footage of my storytelling project *Emerging*, the play *Balm in Gilead*, and all of the films with which I was directly involved: *Gypsy Eyes*, *Cleaning House*, *Infected*, and *525,000 Minutes*. Together, the photographs and videos show the new realities and areas of consciousness that I was about to traverse.

Engaging the Sacred

Ultimately, what unified—and powered—the Morning Pages, as well as the other inspirational tools and techniques that I employed, was one overriding conviction. I set out on the assumption that all things are sacred and interconnected, and I would be open to finding connections between things that I might earlier have thought to be separate. In this way, I would remain consistent with the new science, with a worldview based on spiritual principles, and with the higher dimensions of consciousness that I wished to explore.

I adopted a broad approach to engaging the Sacred and resolved to include Soul and Spirit in all my undertakings. I cultivated a flexibility of mind, allowing that everything can be either real or imagined or both. I would thus welcome rather than fear ambiguity, paradox, uncertainty, and mystery. And in harmony with a worldview that values the knowing of the heart and soul, I would honor the inner world, subjectivity, and concepts of the Divine. I was firm in the belief that ours is a participatory Universe, and that engaging the Sacred would be the key to a personal shift in consciousness that would also assist a wider change in worldview.

Faith in Possibilities

Engaging with the Sacred—being open to the lead of Team Spirit—set me onto a path of unlimited opportunity. I knew deep down that having faith in possibilities would remove the obstacles that might lie ahead of me in my journey of transformation.

In the beginning of my immersion in the arts, I did not know what specific form my transformation might take. But as I turned over the possibilities in my mind, I looked ahead to an adventure that might lead me to the discovery of unexpected life pathways—changing careers, moving to a new location, re-evaluating intimate relationships, and awakening new understanding within my spiritual life. I was open to the new physics' concept of the interconnectedness of all things and the infinity of possibilities that might therefore exist. There is much debate about whether or not the findings of the new physics can be generalized to the outer world. But I had faith that such a leap could indeed be made.

I believed then—as I do now—that what happens within us is reflected in what happens in the outer world, and that there is a oneness beyond the apparent duality in these dimensions. Instead of waiting for science to validate this with certainty, I would simply apply some of the concepts to my own life and person. With my sights set on a new worldview, I pursued my creative projects and took my first steps toward a transformation of consciousness.

three

Emerging—
The Storyteller's Journey

First Test

I had not been enrolled long in my arts immersion program when I realized the path I had chosen would test me at every turn. For the first test, I had to write and perform a personal story from my own experience where I had a realization and went through a major change. The performance was to be short (10 minutes), performed live, solo, and with a minimum of props.

The idea for my story came very quickly. I knew that I wanted to tell the story of my going to acting school full-time at age 45 and emerging as a being whose consciousness had shifted. I wanted to share the conflicts that I had to overcome in order to reinvent my self as a force for changing the worldview. I knew from the start that my struggle would be to release my fear and allow myself to be seen and heard. I also had to relinquish old beliefs about my body, beauty, and sexuality—I now needed to embrace my body as my tool. Most of all, perhaps, to stand fully in my power, I would have to give up my persona of "sympathetic understanding" and integrate all the parts of my femininity—specifically the "virgin" and the "whore." For "the story behind the story," see **Creative Inspiration III**, "An Article Inspired by *Emerging*."

The Dream Connection

I am a dreamer and always take every opportunity to have my inner and outer worlds meet by bringing dreams to life. I do this purposely in order to spark synchronicities—the coming together of related events in a way that often defies rational explanation. Several dreams heralded my entry into acting school and assisted with the story I was now writing. Two of them were especially important. One was my "Butterfly Dream," in which I witnessed myself moving from backstage, through a door, to front and center spotlight on stage—holding a butterfly. The other was a voice dream that told me to "break" my "mask of sympathetic understanding."

The results of my bringing these dreams into "reality" were profound. The "Butterfly" dream gave me a place to begin my story, and added some unique dimensions because the dream (and therefore the eventual performance) included my own conscious witnessing of myself doing the play, from the perspective of just above my right shoulder. This gave me a continual connection to what I was reading in quantum physics about the phenomenon of the "observer." As a result, this dream linked two worlds, bridging the theoretical aspect of my studies and the fieldwork I was doing at school.

The voice dream, "Break Your Mask of Sympathetic Under-standing," showed me the way through my inner conflicts. Performing my story allowed me a chance to create that mask, bring it to form, and then actually remove it as other people witnessed. I recorded the event in my Morning Pages:

> One of the very first lessons I learned about myself in acting school was that over my years of training and practicing as a therapist, I had developed a "mask of sympathetic understanding" . . . I began to see how stuck I was in a particular way of interacting with people, a way in which I listen, I hear, I understand, and I share nothing of what goes on inside me. It was a way I had developed to move in the world that had led me from one unsatisfying caretaking relationship to another in my personal life. It was a way of being that left me crying out inside, wishing to be seen and heard, yet unable to even recognize that I had on a mask that prevented this.

While this way of being assisted me tremendously in my work as a therapist and teacher, it only hindered me as an actress. When filmed on camera, the feedback from my teachers was usually that I needed to relax, to put more of myself forward, and to allow more of how I was feeling to come through my eyes.

It was this latter feedback that shocked me the most, particularly when I saw myself on the screen. I knew what I was feeling, what my intention was, yet I could see that none of what was going on inside me was coming through in my eyes. I had a shield up, a shield I had developed over the years as a therapist to enable me to conceal my true feelings and meet any "shocking" or "horrifying" story with a warm and sympathetic gaze.

One of the first tasks that I had to do in order to increase my effectiveness as a performer was to release my guard, to open up and allow my very soul essence to be truthfully expressed in order that I could actually be seen.

The work that I performed in Storytelling, where I actually created my mask and then removed it while the audience witnessed my emergence, changed something. I let my inner conflict be seen and declared that I was now going to: 1) acknowledge and work with my body as a tool; 2) allow myself to be seen and heard; and 3) allow myself to acknowledge and work with my beauty . . . After that, I was aware of my mask of sympathetic understanding and my "eye guard" when I did scenes. I am now capable of both putting them on and taking them off as the situation calls for.

There has been an impact on my personal relationships as well. For example, I have ended and/or changed the dynamics of personal relationships that had become based on caretaking. This will remain an element of my relationships that I continue to be highly conscious of.

Throughout my journey as a storyteller, my dream connections sparked ideas and allowed me to change my mind about who I was and what I was capable of doing. There was often a synchronicity between my dreams and my continuing research into the nature of consciousness. I had been reading about how possibilities can co-exist and the metaphor of the butterfly provided a case in point. As I wrote in my Morning Pages, "I am the larva; I am the chrysalis; I am the butterfly. All exist as possibilities simultaneously." At this point, I realized that the experience of going through fine arts school was not simply about transforming me. It was about connecting with different ideas in order that parts of me that were already there could emerge. I now had my story's title: *Emerging*.

Another interesting thing happened. One day a fellow student brought in research she had done for me, unsolicited. She had looked up the symbolic meaning of butterflies, and her findings were a sign that I was on the right path. Across many cultures and centuries, the butterfly has endured as an ultimate emblem of transformative power.

Truth, Freedom, and Choice

During the creation of *Emerging* I did a lot of research on beauty, aesthetics, and freedom, since these subjects were linked to the themes of the story. I made an interesting connection between truth and freedom, which even connected with acting. "The art of acting," I wrote in my Morning Pages, "is to express truth even in imaginary situations and to be able to connect with truth. This, in and of itself, leads to freedom."

When I thought about the story I was writing and the changes I was undergoing, I also realized that the only true freedom is the freedom of choice. As always, my Morning Pages enabled me to articulate my new understanding:

> This is the gift. I have the ability to choose and I choose to be beautiful; I choose to express the beauty of my soul; I choose to free myself from old thoughts, old beliefs, old patterns; I choose to change my thoughts; I choose to express Higher Truths; I choose attitudes that attract High Vibrational Fields. No one is stopping me . . . and

I choose to make the changes that align me more closely with my power.

> I no longer *wish* . . . I am resolved . . . My character goes from wishing to resolving. With this I am given great strength. My destiny is solely within the power of my own hands . . . it is the consequence of my choices.

My reflections on truth soon led me to yet another insight. It was not enough just to tell the truth—it must be expressed properly in order to be accepted. I realized that I needed to present my story in a way that the audience would grasp and relate to. And, as I ex-pressed it in my Morning Pages, proper presentation entailed accepting responsibility for my choices, decisions, and their consequences: "I know that my decisions ripple through the universe of consciousness to affect the lives of all . . . that every act, thought, and choice adds to a permanent mosaic. My decisions support life. The ripples I create return to me." In my journey as a storyteller, I had now gone far enough to see that who I allowed myself to be would largely determine the level to which truth would reach the audience, and possibly shift people.

In other words, in order for the play to truly move others, I must be the butterfly. And, one day, life put me to just such a test. Would I be willing to make myself seen and heard? Would I be the butterfly?

I had written the outline of my story and had taken much care with it; however, I needed to miss the class on the day it was to be presented, so I really wanted my teacher to review my written work instead. When I was giving it to him, he responded by telling me to keep it, that when I came to class I would read the story and he would go through it then. But I had worked hard all weekend on completing this project. I was really happy with my work. I liked it. I wanted him to see it. After humming and hawing for a while, I said to him, "Here. Just have it."

He quickly glanced through as he began making excuses like, "Well, I'll read it over." Then I saw him stop and really look at one of the pages. "Wow. This is well written. I'll use this as an example in my classes," he said. I was grateful.

My "guts" were turning for a long time after that encounter—and then I realized that I had been tested. "Be seen and be heard." I had passed the test. I had wanted him to read my script. Usually I would have just kept my work, said nothing, and been disappointed. But not Butterfly Woman. Butterfly Woman got her work looked at, even if only briefly. I ensured that my voice was heard—my writing, seen.

The Power of Simplicity

As the storytelling course continued, I progressed from story outline to actual script. Writing the first draft of the script at home by myself was a wonderful, joyful experience. Then I took it out into the world and gave my first reading in class.

The day after, I wrote in my Morning Pages:

> This is so funny. I did my first read today of my actual script. I am surprised by the feedback. The teacher said, "Can you put some of the language into simpler language . . . for example, does everyone here know what a 'prophetic' dream is?"
>
> To my surprise many of the students did not know what the word meant.
>
> This is a word I use all the time. Being with this class, this class of teenagers, I realize how much in an ivory tower I actually have been. Just like in the play, I have been tucked away . . . and in a way I can no longer relate.
>
> I never think of myself as speaking intellectually, yet I can remember being told this before. I remember one woman commenting on the way I speak, "Wow. She speaks in full sentences."
>
> I am realizing that the stuff I am studying, the areas I am interested in . . . they are so far out there for so many people. This class really brings that into sharp reality.
>
> And I have a conflict. Part of me wants to keep my own voice . . . a voice which is scholarly. Yet . . . if I don't

reach the audience . . . so what if I keep my voice? What good is that if people don't understand me?

Me: "But some people would understand me."

Inner Voice: "Be real. Most of the audience here is going to be teens. Speak to them."

I used to think that I wanted to reach the general population with my work. My friend used to ask me why. He used to say that I needed a more distinguished, sophisticated, intellectual audience. I used to argue vehemently. I used to argue that my intention was to reach the masses.

What my writing process during *Emerging* taught me was that if I were going to reach the masses and the youth, I would have to clean up my language. I needed to simplify so that anyone could understand the message. It took a lot of work but the end result was a shorter, simpler, and more effective final draft; it is reproduced in this book as **Creative Inspiration IV.**

The Sign of the Butterfly

One very special moment happened just after the first reading of my script. This confirmed for me that I was on the right track and gave me faith to persist with the story.

My main intention in sharing this story with others was to inspire them, but I had never told the class this. At the end of class, one of the students, who is also a painter, came up to me and gave me the picture that had flashed into her head as I read my story, and which she had doodled onto the front page of my script. On the doodle she wrote: "Duanita, you've inspired a painting. That doesn't happen very often. This painting will be for you."

I took this as a sign that the intention of my story, "to inspire," was being felt. I was on the right track. This was in fact the first among several conscious intentions that I set and worked with during the creation of *Emerging*; see **Creative Inspiration V.**

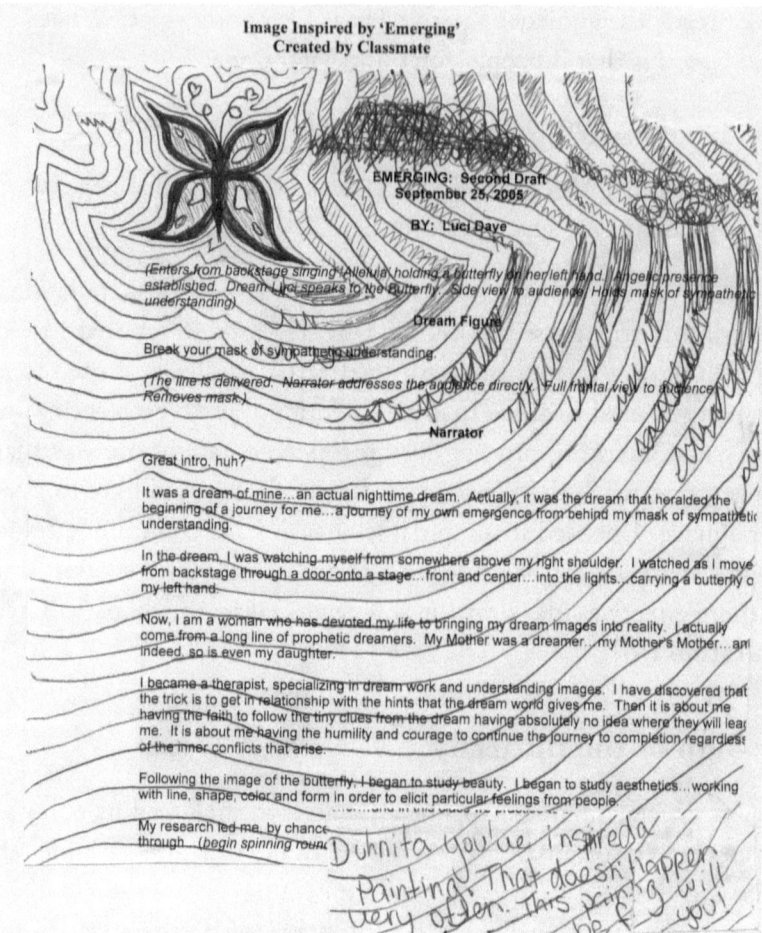

Image Inspired by 'Emerging'
Created by Classmate

Interacting with Characters and Self

One of the biggest boons of taking acting classes was how much easier it became for me to develop characters during the script-writing process. The creation of the characters for *Emerging* was a very intriguing process, because they were all parts of me that I had to explore, identify, and bring to life. I began by writing the characters' biographies. Then I worked in my Morning Pages with active imagination—that is, asking some questions and seeing how the characters revealed themselves.

One of the characters I created is the Acting Teacher. In the story, she is a somewhat comic muse who teaches through humor and serves as a reminder that the responsibility of the actor is to be seen and heard. The teacher takes a dim view of another character, Sister Marie. The nun is repressed, moralistic, judgmental, and often fearful. She stands up sternly for right—but not necessarily the kind of right that promotes positive change and joy.

Bambii—with two i's, as she is apt to point out—is the polar opposite of the nun. A sensual woman and free spirit, Bambii is more than capable of speaking up for herself:

> I move with my hips and I turn my shoulders . . . I even move my shoulders . . . I am street smart when I am you. I have been judged—condemned . . . well . . . that sounds like something you would do. I would be with a man—do a one-night stand, brush men off, never settle down, tease with my body. I know how beautiful I am. I know how sexy I am. And I am pissed that I have never been fully recognized. I have never been allowed to really come out on a continual basis . . . only on special occasions. I am very brave because despite the judgment, I carry on— knowing I am beautiful; knowing that men want me; knowing that they are afraid of so much woman; knowing that the world is mine.

Sister Marie and Bambii are in fact two sides of the main character Luci, a highly competent therapist who aspires to being an actress. In creating Luci, I was really developing a profile of myself, or at least the part of myself that was my core persona at the time. This whole process of paying serious attention to all the parts of myself made me marvel at the ways I was changing my consciousness—simply through observing and reflecting on my inner conflicts and myself.

Creation of the Mask

As a direct result of my voice dream and work on the story, I decided to artistically craft my "mask of sympathetic understanding." I formed it right on my face using plaster bandages; I then sprayed it gold. As I created the physical mask, I explored its meaning in my Morning Pages:

31

Part of me is scared, you know, really scared. Can I actually do it? Can I actually perform . . . in front of people . . . show them what is really inside of me . . . reveal myself . . . be honest about who I really am?

I am scared. I choke. I write this great play, this great script, and I question my ability to pull it off. I am so used to hiding. I am so used to remaining unseen.

This mask has gotten me far . . . but it also has gotten me in trouble. I have denied myself and denied my voice. And I haven't done anyone any favors in doing so. In failing to reveal my truth, I have failed to take responsibility for the gifts that I was born with. My fear has blocked me from being a steward of my beauty, my brains, my body, my voice, my intuition, my connection to my dreams . . . and moving these into the arena of life where they can play.

I also explored what it meant for me to consider releasing myself from behind the mask:

This shame thing. I think that I feel some shame. I am ashamed of myself for having such thoughts. I am ashamed of myself for having a spirit that needs to break free. Part of me would so love it if I just had the consciousness that would allow me to be a nun. I could stay in my cocoon, nice and safe, and never have to come out. And I would please others. Breaking through . . . being different is difficult. I find it lonely actually. The more I move and learn and grow, the less I fit in my old worlds.

This brought up a lot of fear about what would happen to me if I actually took a risk and became a performer:

Starting all over again! I feel like I have been starting all over again all my life—breaking rules, challenging norms all my life . . . and that was when I was behind my mask of sympathetic understanding!

What truly are the implications of breaking this mask, dropping this persona? I am afraid that I won't be able to be a therapist anymore. What if I have to give up my work—my livelihood? What then? What if it is stupid? What if I make a fool out of myself? What if it isn't really great or meaningful? What if it calibrates really low?

I am especially afraid of having people there that know me. I feel I can do it for strangers because I don't care what they think. It is the people I know that scare me.

In class, synchronistically, we were working with masks and learning the traditions of masks in theater. We were asked to do an exercise. Five students lined up behind chairs that held the masks that we had made, including my mask of sympathetic understanding. We were then told to put our masks on ritually, which meant that we turned away from the audience, breathed out, and then placed the masks on our faces. When we turned back to the audience we were each the character of the mask—transformed. After putting the masks on, we then moved with emotion. In succession, each of the five students put on the various masks.

The result of this exercise was a very powerful realization. I recognized that when I put on the mask of sympathetic understanding, I felt very powerful. I feel powerful when no one can see me. I was actually smiling behind the mask. This generated a question. Was part of my resistance to being seen and heard a fear of losing some of my power?

When I looked at the mask on others and allowed it to speak to me, it spoke of pain and sadness. When I had it on and looked at people, I saw fear in their eyes. I would smile to alleviate their fear and then realize that they could not see my smile behind the mask.

The creation of the mask of sympathetic understanding was a turning point and became a strong influence in the development of the play. Once the mask existed, I knew that it needed to be part of the performance of my story. With this idea came the decision to work with more masks to designate the other parts of myself as well. The one exception was my true self, which is revealed right at the end of the story when all the parts of myself come together to remove the mask of sympathetic understanding.

Suddenly, my performance had become one of mask work, which in the tradition of the theater is sacred. I was moving forward in my journey. And at the same time, in the way of oneness, I was living my beginning assumption that all things are sacred.

four

Feeling the Sacred

A Sacred Piece

I was now at the rehearsal phase of *Emerging*. I was getting better at speaking up for myself, and now I had yet another important lesson to learn: the need to speak up for the Sacred. I was confronted with a situation where I needed to make a stand on behalf of my masks, which I had lovingly, and in a sacred manner, prepared and endowed with a life of their own. I recorded a full accounting of the incident in my Morning Pages:

> At dress rehearsal my ability to speak up for the Sacred was tested. One of the students was fooling around during break. She asked me for my masks. Inside my head the conversation was quick:
>
> *"My masks?! My masks are preparing for a presentation. Didn't she get the <u>sacred</u> part of masks that the teacher was very careful to emphasize? I don't want to let her play with my masks."*
>
> Instead of speaking up for myself and the masks, however, I said in my usual "don't get-anyone-mad-at-me, avoid-the-question" kind of way: "Oh I don't know where they are." I lied. I knew exactly where they were. I had been very careful to put them under a chair so that no one would step on them accidentally.

Immediately I felt guilty for not protecting them. I had been working so hard on trusting myself to protect myself, and here again I was not saying what I needed to say because I could not believe this student did not get the message in class about how we treat masks. I didn't want to hurt her feelings, to make her feel stupid. So I gave up my power and instead of speaking my truth, I lied.

I was surprised and relieved to hear my teacher (who had overheard her ask me for the masks) say, "You can't use someone's sacred masks."

"*Wow*," I thought. "*He got it. He protected me. He understood the sacredness of my play, of my story. The ritual.*"

I thought the matter was done.

A moment later I heard, "Oh there's the box." I watched as this student ran over to the box with my masks under the chair. I felt powerless. I watched in amazement as she went through the box, picked out the Sister Marie/ Bambii mask, put it on and proceed to play with it.

I felt sick to my stomach. This is the young woman I had been thinking about getting to help me paint the cross on the forehead of the Sister Marie mask. In that moment, I realized how wrong I had been about her. I realized that she had no understanding of the sacred nature of performance masks, even though one teacher had taught it clearly and another had warned her.

I realized in that moment that I needed to paint the cross myself. I realized that I needed to really get into my power and that I had to speak up for myself and for my masks. Affirmations went off in my head: "*I trust myself to speak out and ask for what I need . . . STOP PEOPLE!!!*"

This incident, the violation of masks, really impacted me. I was truly upset at my failure to speak. I recognized patterns in myself and took full responsibility for what had happened. Indeed, how could I be heard if I failed to speak, especially when the issue was so extremely important?

I was also truly upset about the fact that this incident had happened at all. The teachers had been so careful to teach us about the sacredness of mask work. Why had the message failed to be transmitted to this student?

As I agonized later over this whole incident, I had a profound realization. I realized that my story, *Emerging*, was a sacred piece. Though I had known this before when I was writing it, I guess I had never truly *felt* it, until the violation happened. When the sacred nature of the masks was threatened, something shifted in me. I *felt* the sacredness of the play, the writing, the music, and I *felt* moved to protect it.

This new perspective changed many things. For example, previous to this shift, I felt apologetic about singing "Alleluia" during my entrance. I even felt apologetic about doing the chant "We All Come From the Mother." I had learned "Alleluia" as part of the Ukrainian Catholic Mass in which I had participated as a child. The chant I had learned from a medicine woman two decades prior. I felt shaky incorporating them into my story and performing them on stage. I felt they were not "modern" enough for the young crowd, and that they would not be able to relate to them. In some ways, to sing these songs almost seemed sacrilegious. When the "shift" happened inside me, however, suddenly it felt right to work with these songs. I realized that this was my journey—and that my journey of emerging was a sacred process—and these songs were sacred to me.

I developed a deeper understanding of how creativity itself is sacred and how, indeed, emerging into fuller consciousness is a sacred transition.

Sacred—and Scared

At the very first class rehearsal, when I went to make a move as my character Bambii, someone made a "catcall" whistle in the audience. My physical and emotional reaction was extreme.

I totally lost my concentration. I had to ad lib Bambii and Sister Marie. I was no longer in control. Inside of me a conversation was taking place: *"Just keep going! What do I say?"* I was in a different part of my brain. I knew that I just had to trust myself. My body moved automatically, pivoting as I changed characters. I had to remember what the last character said. They weren't saying what was on the script. I had to take a beat and listen and process what the other character had said. Then I had to put in what the most important point of that part of the conversation was, as I was unable to cognitively remember the script.

It was scary. The writer in me was screaming *"Lines, line! That part— that word—was so important. It was the transition line. How could you miss it?"* I was helpless inside as Bambii and Sister Marie took over. Sister Marie was shocked at the catcall. She was speechless and it came across in her voice. Sister Marie also felt real fear of Bambii at this point. I felt her back down—and, actually, in this play she does have to back down.

Bambii was also surprised at Sister Marie's lack of words. She had won—and, honestly, I needed to slow down and take a beat here because Bambii also did not know what to say. Here is where I learned how important it is to trust myself as a person and as an actor. If I trust myself, I can move out of the way and allow the characters to come through. After the first dress rehearsal, a student that I knew only slightly gave me a very precious gift. Up to this point in time, whenever I asked my regular classmates what they got from my story, I heard, "Scared. It made me scared."

I had already changed the language of the script, because in the first version they did not understand many of the words I had used. I had also totally changed two of my characters because classmates had found them too "angry" and the anger "scared" them. I had altered Bambii and made her sensuous, and I had made Sister Marie reserved. I was tired of their fear and finally just asked them, "But do you guys get the message? That we are all one?"

"No," was the resounding answer.

My main intention—to inspire the audience, to help them feel that connection, that oneness—was obviously not coming through. One sharp student did say, "Well . . . I see your story like it is all parts of you and you get it together . . . and like we can all do that." This response was a glimmer of hope for me.

Then, after the first dress rehearsal, this student I hardly knew casually commented to me, "Wow . . . your play is very deep."

I thought, "*Oh my God—somebody sees that.*" I was very excited.

"Yes . . . it's like we all have these parts in us," he said as he mulled his thoughts. "Yes. The inner critic—the part that says, 'You can't do it: No one wants to listen.' Yes. I do that. I think too much."

I was surprised for a moment, because I realized that this was a young man who was identifying with my character. I said, "Yes, and then we have the Rebel."

"Yes . . . it is like a constant conflict in my head. Outside of the school I can be intellectual . . . inside here, it is Bambii," he said. He got quiet.

"Yes . . . and the trick is to get them working together . . . it is in the oneness that the power is," I responded.

"Yes . . . but that's hard," he said.

"Indeed. It is," I agreed.

I was so grateful for this gift. The message for me was that the deep message I was giving could be consciously understood. I could be truly heard—truly seen.

Working with Atmospheres

My work on *Emerging* was to show the "oneness" of all the different parts of the individual, as well as to reflect that which connects everyone and everything in all states of consciousness. For this play I therefore had an intention to create in the room an atmosphere of "oneness." My Morning Pages hold a record of a profound experience I had:

> I must say, God . . . I am so grateful . . . I felt it yesterday. I felt the inner image become more real than the outer. In class yesterday, I was watching the scenes and then I realized that my vision had totally blurred and that my eyes were unblinking. I was aware of the nearness of the teacher and I felt my body go alive . . . my lower chakras in particular. I could feel us merging . . . and I heard him saying, "See . . . this is what I mean by holding the feeling . . . do you feel that?" Yes . . . yes I do feel that. An atmosphere of oneness . . . of total connection. Now . . . just imagine . . . you know that this is happening with

everyone and everything . . . throughout time . . . this is the atmosphere of oneness that I bring to my story . . . the truth of oneness.

It seems to me that an actor's skill is to tap into the alternate atmospheres available . . . by holding the feeling. This draws the reality into existence . . . for me and everyone in the room . . . in the world, actually. And the more power I bring to the world . . . the more I bet it counteracts ignorance.

Now . . . this last part is important . . . because I was originally thinking to use line, shape, and color to elicit particular feelings . . . and yes . . . that is part of it . . . to elicit feelings of love, joy, elation . . . inspiration . . . and the other component is that I must *feel* it . . . it must come through me . . . I must *BE* it.

I began to seriously work with the concept of "atmosphere" and began to identify, imagine, and fully "feel" different atmospheres around me. I began consciously endeavoring to create energy fields, which would then give me something to move up against as an actor and allow me to act more easily.

I began rehearsing different atmospheres for the play in my mind— deeply concentrating, observing, and creating the flow of these atmospheres in my head. In my Morning Pages, I described this flow of atmospheres, which I worked on layering into the story. I wrote "as if" I were doing it during my performance:

1. Angelic, Heavenly, Inspiring, Spiritual, Creative Atmosphere. This is the atmosphere that holds together the play. I create this atmosphere before I even walk into the room. I create it daily every moment of every day. I see the space absolutely filled with angels. I see the crowd inspired . . . on their feet . . . deeply moved to create . . . to be inspired to live their dreams, create, take risks, and follow their dreams. I see the room absolutely sparkling with magic . . . I see the quantum field and energy circuits

come alive. I see myself as huge, big . . . absolutely filling the room with love, peace, joy, and enlightenment . . . the calibrations as Dr. Hawkins depicts them, coming off of me, soaring in the 600s and beyond.

Now . . . this is the atmosphere that is the container for the entire play. It begins before I am there and then is ignited before I go onstage . . . when I become the Angel coming in with the observer . . . with God or the Great Creator right there observing this whole thing into being. I meld my will with the Will of the observer at that point . . . and this is the point where the door to all of the quantum possibilities flies open.

After I lead the audience through the other atmospheres . . . I end back in heaven . . . and create another bit of heaven for them. They have, at that point, witnessed my journey through my blocks of fear, self-criticism, and coming to the importance of oneness. I am radiating . . . love, joy, happiness. I am inspired and I lift them . . . to the ecstasy of new birth.

2. The second atmosphere is that of intense connection. Boom . . . heaven is around us . . . and I explain that in the present. I engage them . . . I connect all of their hearts with my own cord and I then take them into the usual world of acting school.

3. The third atmosphere is jovial—fun, smiling, laughter . . . to the extreme . . . over the top . . . and they love this jester and they connect with her. They have fun with her.

4. The fourth atmosphere is inner conflict. I want to remove the mask and play and create. I have a battle between fear and anger. The feeling is anguish . . . until I break . . .

5. The fifth atmosphere is *empowerment* . . . and this is the core. As I move the parts of myself together (focused positively in a creative direction), I realize my power. I align with the Will of God and am able to actualize the dream reality. I find my power and then bring the audience back to a light heaven, reminding them that they too are part of this oneness.

I began playing with the atmosphere of coming into my power at the end, through my critical movement. When my teacher brought up the issue of my power as an actor, I realized the importance of this. I realized that I must fully embrace my power, in the play and in this phase of my life. I must fully turn on and connect with my power and, actually, it is a power far greater than mine. This is the power that comes from the Observer—which comes from that part of me that sits above my right shoulder watching me do this—watching me create. It is about connecting with this part and aligning my will with it and creating.

The power that the audience experiences is not my power. It is the power of creative energy that runs through me, that runs through them. It is not my power that they are frightened of—it is their power, the experience of *their* own connection with Divine creativity, with Creative Energy.

All About Audience

Through my creative process with this story, I learned that performance is all about the audience. As one of my teachers said, "It's all just fooling around until it is performed in front of the audience." Here again is the importance of being seen, of being observed into being. With an audience, I had witnesses to my process. This created a whole different experience for me, because it became about the exchange of energy between the audience and me. I put out my story of EMERGING. They witness it and energy is shifted in them. I wit-ness this and it changes me as I emerge.

The example of the catcall during rehearsals is a case in point. Through this experience, I got to *feel* what it would be like to have men appreciate me or regard me as sexy. I felt that whistle reverberate in my body and I felt a chemical reaction take place. All sorts of emotions were triggered—

elation, surprise, shock, shame, fear, joy. It is this type of experience that grounds my knowledge that I can reinvent myself, that I am capable of performing "magic."

My Morning Pages also reflect an insight I had into the connection of the material with the audience:

> My teacher said something yesterday which I found very intriguing. He said, "Storytelling doesn't happen on stage. It happens at the back of the audience's heads." I love this image. You see, this story isn't even what it is really about. It is about the connection of the audience members with their own power, their own creativity . . . their connection with God, the Great Creator, the great Creative Spirit that stirs in them. They are inspired to do something, to take a risk . . . to bring their dreams into reality.

The script was together, the costume and masks were made, and the final rehearsals were set. The teacher asked us to think about how many people we would invite to the performance to ensure that the venue would be adequate. I found myself conflicted between my fear of letting myself be seen and heard, and my true desire to have the courage to show the world my inner life.

I decided to tell no one about my performance, to just have strangers in the audience. About one week before the performance, however, I was driving home from school and realized that part of the challenge I was facing included sharing my experience with people I knew. It meant inviting them to the performance. I was being called, after all, to be seen and to be heard. So I phoned my friends on the cell from the car and invited them before I had a chance to talk myself out of it.

On the night of my performance, five of my closest friends came and saw what I was doing. I am grateful that they did. Performing in front of strangers would have been much easier for me but, somehow, having the courage to be seen in this new light by my friends more deeply and permanently solidified the lessons I was learning. This connects to the whole idea in quantum physics that something needs to be seen before it can be "popped" into reality and that, in the mere act of seeing it, whatever is observed is changed.

Duanita G. Eleniak, PhD

Encouragement and Empowerment

A month or so before the performance, I had a dream about my being in acting school: *I am in school and I am saying that I am grateful to do this in my 40s because I get in just under the wire . . . just when I can still really enjoy it.*

This dream helped alleviate some of the concerns that were coming up for me during the storytelling process. I kept wondering why I was there. What was I doing in acting school with 11 youngsters when I was in my 40s? The dream seemed to suggest that my reason for being there was simply sheer enjoyment and that I was there just at the right time. All I had to do was to be grateful for the opportunity that I had wanted for so long—that is, to be able to go back to school full-time once again.

A few nights later, I had a dream that also encouraged me and gave me renewed energy to stay on path regarding my story, *Emerging: I am reading fan mail. I read this one handwritten letter from the local priest. He is crying as he tells me he saw an angel during my performance (I am not sure if he meant it was me or a real Angel). He was obviously extremely moved. Then I read another that has a side note: "You are a great writer."*

Creating *Emerging* gave these dreams an opportunity to be expressed; and this resulted in a reaffirmation of the power of dreams to encourage me, to help me continue creating, and to sustain faith in my process. My dream life became an integral part of my creative process. My first semi-full-dress rehearsal of the story was also encouraging. More important, the feedback I received gave me insights about power. When I wrote in my Morning Pages the next day, I noted that as I walked onto the stage, my finger holding the butterfly was I would say that everything is working OK, except for my characters of Bambii and Sister Marie. Sister Marie came out angry and Bambii was *really* angry. The Nun is to be quiet, pious, and reserved. She is an expression of the inner fear that holds me back. Bambii is supposed to be sensuous, sexy . . . too sexy for her dress.

Anyhow, I did the presentation and then came the feedback. The teacher said he was scared, taken aback, and he asked the students if they felt the same thing. He said, "It is a powerful piece. You are very powerful. I don't think you realize how powerful you are . . . especially with the masks."

This whole issue of power intrigued me and even bothered me a bit. I found myself teetering on the verge of anger as I relived the rehearsal in my Morning Pages:

> You see, I have seen people be afraid of me when I stand fully in my power. Indeed, my mask, the mask of sympathetic understanding, the mask that the dream world has asked me to remove, well, in class, a majority of the students were scared of it. Only one was "intrigued." And I guess I have for a long time had this reaction from men that I am intimate with and even with some friends. When I fully move into my power, they are frightened. And this makes me angry. It makes me angry that I cannot fully express myself. It makes me angry that they can express themselves . . . and yet I am not allowed to. My loud voice scares them. Huh!
>
> Well . . . for a moment after getting that feedback, I was angry and I doubted myself. I wondered, "Do I need to turn down the volume of power in this play?" And my inner answer came very strong. "No! This is a stage . . . and on this stage I am fully able to reveal my power."

As a result of this dress rehearsal and doing this play, I *realized* my power. I was able to see that the story I was telling about myself was also about my fully claiming and living in my power while connecting with a Power far greater than I.

As the evening of the performance approached, I continued what had become an important daily practice. In my Morning Pages, I would write out my adapted version of the Artist's Prayer and contemplate it alone each morning before I went to school. This renewed my appreciation of the power of prayer and helped me feel less lonely. Even without a physical peer group of artists supporting me as I created *Emerging*, when I worked with the prayer, I realized that I was connected with each and every other artist in the world (alive and dead) who had struggled as I had.

The prayer also gave me more of a sense of community with my fellow students. It helped me continue to recognize on a daily basis that we were all in this together, moving through to the best of our abilities. To be reminded of my connection with community was especially important at the point in my process where I became disheartened. I had lost heart, lost courage, because no one seemed to understand my words, my vocabulary, my symbolism, or what I was trying to say. The prayer gave me the faith to keep going.

In writing out the prayer everyday, I felt spontaneous connections enter my head, and I would allow these to flow down to the page. Often they would bring deeper insight into an element of what I was creating. For example, in the middle of writing out the Artist's Prayer a few days before the performance, the following "blurt" came through, along with new insight and perspective.

> We open to our creativity in our lives. We surrender to you our old ideas . . . especially mine around money, fear, and sympathetic understanding. I am seeing . . . truly seeing . . . how this mask I wore has hurt me over the years. I so much never wanted to do anything to hurt anyone . . . and I ended up hurting myself.

Preparation for the Performance

In addition to adding finishing touches to script, character, intention, and atmosphere, the day of the performance also included having my hair, makeup, and nails done. While talking with my hairstylist, I had a flash of enlightenment that I later recalled in my Morning Pages:

> My stylist asked me a question about whether I found myself competing with my classmates. I said, "Well, most of them are 18 and 19 years old. And some of them don't work very hard." And you know, I realized that this was very true. Most of them struggled with being off book by the deadline or having their black binders or scripts ready. Actually, a lot of time was wasted by people not being there or being unprepared. I realized (as I told my stylist) that what I would really like is to be part of is a group

of really hot actors/artists, who are hard-working—who do their work—who de-bate the finer points of acting with me . . . so that I can discuss the atmospheres I am creating, the empowering of my masks . . . go more into detail rather than just get the play up. In this group I have done the latter all by myself . . . with the very little information that I have learned in my classes and through my own reading.

It used to be that I apologized for my high standards . . . like hiding my top grades all through high school as a kid to avoid being labelled a "nerd" . . . to have people like me. Well, I refuse to do that anymore. I am willing to do what it takes to excel as an artist and I begin now. I no longer sacrifice my brilliance to make others feel better.

I even found a quote on the official Sophia Loren website to strengthen this conviction: "I was blessed with a sense of my own destiny. I have never sold myself short. I have never judged myself by other people's standards. I have always expected a great deal of myself, and if I fail, I fail myself." This insight reflected me as an artist fully standing in my power, willing to be seen and heard and to do everything in my power to shine as brightly as I possibly could. Somehow the process that I had already been through, just in the creation of this story, had resulted in a shift of consciousness for me.

The resolve that fell into place during this hair appointment was that I would continue to work to the absolute best of my abilities, regardless of the artists in whose company I found myself. In other words, instead of being motivated by "competition" (the state of consciousness assumed by the hairdresser and promoted in the current dominant worldview), I would be motivated by my desire to reinvent myself into the very best instrument possible, through which Creative Energy could flow. I resolved to use my gifts to the fullest in the expression of the Creative Force, for the purpose of bringing forth a reality where love, peace, joy, and integrity are common human values, and we as people remember the connection between the inner and outer realms.

In retrospect, I can see that I had in fact formulated such a resolve very early in the program—and consistently performed at my highest level of excellence, regardless of what my fellow artists were doing. I was always prepared for my scenes to the very best of my ability. I showed up for classes and was there promptly with few exceptions. I listened to tapes and, as much as possible, educated myself beyond the requirements of the school.

The result of my hard work and desire to be the very best that I could be had interesting effects, particularly with regard to the perceptions of my fellow students. On one occasion at the end of the program, I was in my teacher's office making copies of my work. To my surprise, he said, "Your classmate thinks you are an alien, you know?" I was taken aback by the comment and began to laugh.

"No, he truly, honestly believes you are an alien because he cannot see how there could be any other way that you could always come to class, be prepared, and do all the other things that you do unless you were one," my teacher said.

Though I laughed off the comment at the time, I was intrigued to hear of this perception of me. This was exactly the reason why I had hidden my light for so many years—I was afraid that I would not fit in. The difference now was that I had stopped caring about being seen as "different" or "in a class of my own." I was fine with being seen as "alien."

Just before my performance of *Emerging*, another insight came to me as a result of reading the section on "Shame" in Julia Cameron's book, *The Artist's Way* (1992): "We must learn that when our art reveals a secret of the human soul, those watching it may try to shame us for making it." Cameron talks about how shame prevents us from putting our work out, whether it be childhood shame or shaming by critics. I realized that shame may be one of the biggest reasons why I have never really put my creative work out in the world, especially since a lot of it has to do with sexuality.

I began to do affirmations to release this shame. I dedicated myself to what Cameron identified as "the antidote to the shaming": self-love and self-praise. I committed to healing from all the shaming in my life. I knew that I just needed to perform and to show up and to look for no one's approval but my own.

After reading about the effects of shame, I had a dream: *I needed to rehearse my story; however, I needed to do so in my underwear. I was very upset because I had not yet got new underwear and my old one was worn out with bobbles on the breasts.* I felt ashamed in the dream, ashamed of my underwear, and I later realized that this dream was a reality. None of my bras were looking good under my new dress. I had hesitated at buying new underwear and had attempted to piecemeal it together. I concluded that getting new underwear was essential.

I expressed gratitude for the dream. I knew I had nothing to be ashamed of. I was ready to perform my story.

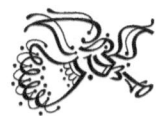

five

A Heart-Stopping Performance— and the Aftermath

Brush with Death

My story was a story of rebirth—a dying of the old me and a rebirth of the new me—the death of me as a therapist and the rebirth of me as an artist. And on stage that night, I had a literal brush with death. My heart gave out.

I have trouble with my heart. I get times when my heart begins "sucking" rather than pumping. In order to get it to beat again, I have discovered that I must hold my breath. I have eliminated caffeine, alcohol, drugs, nicotine, and begun a really healthy lifestyle and diet in order to deal with this; however, once in a while, it still happens.

The moment that it decided to happen was during the first night of my performance, right when I began doing the character of the Acting Teacher. During dress rehearsals, I never fully reached the energy level of performance. When I did that night, my heart began sucking while I was onstage.

Inside, I was thinking, *"What if I drop dead here on stage? People will think it is part of the act! Who will call 911?"*

I kept going. I felt my arms go weak. I had trouble concentrating on the words of the story. It was as if I were on automatic pilot. I was grateful for all the preparation I had done beforehand, because the audience had no conscious idea of what I was going through physically or emotionally on the inside. The most that they noticed was that my singing voice was shaky. They had no idea that it was because I could not catch my breath.

When I finished my performance, my head was splitting. I could see auras around all lights. I felt nauseated. Every muscle in my body hurt. My heart began pumping again.

I went through an actual death experience in my inner world on that first night that I performed my story of rebirth, *Emerging.* To this day I wonder how this inner experience (even if the audience was unaware of it on a conscious level) impacted the atmosphere, the audience? Did it heighten an atmosphere of rebirth, of suspense with regard to whether or not I would move through? Could they sense my inner panic?

I was very excited to see this performance on film in order to watch myself go through a literal death experience on the inside while sharing a rebirth story on the outside. As it turns out, the camera disappeared that night. Stolen? Maybe. But whatever happened to it, the visual record of my experience remained only in the minds of audience members. (A DVD of another performance of *Emerging* is available. See **Resources** at the back of this book.)

After the Performance

My only formal "grading" on this project came from a dream I had shortly afterward: *I am in acting school. The project grades are in. They put it in our purse. I go and look at the paper and see that I got 33/35. I begin to read through the comments.*

My Morning Pages from the day after the performance capture the comments that I personally received from audience members that night:

"I was floored." (acting teacher)

"I cried." (two people)

"It made me see that often I live in the old part of me."

"It was very deep . . . there was depth and complexity that drew you in."

"It was most creative."

"What you did moved everyone forward . . . to the next step." (an acting instructor) I asked him what he meant by this. I think he was implying that I inspired people to take their work to the next level, but I remain unsure.

"That woman took a huge step forward." (psychologist of one of the students who saw the performance told this to the student)

"That took guts. That took a lot of guts."

"The sheer passion that you had . . ."

"You never held back."

"It was moving. It moved people."

"I was touched. I was moved. I cried."

"You were beautiful the other night. You had me on the floor. The best part was watching your daughter's response."

"You're hot." (over and over again)

"I want Duanita's body when I'm 45."

"My Dad is sooo gonna love you."

"Hmmmmm." (from a gay man)

One of the men from the school did not recognize me when he first saw me dressed for the performance. When he did, he said, "Break a leg." I said, "Thank you." He said, "No . . . thank yoooouuuu," in appreciation of my physical beauty, I think.

Healing and Realizations

Performing my story and hearing the feedback brought me to a point of profound personal healing. I reflected in the following passage from my Morning Pages:

I have realized that doing this play—creating the play and performing it—is part of my healing. I have been *blind* to the importance of the visual, to my beauty, and to the power of beauty. Actually, blind is probably the wrong word because I can see it and I can see other women using it. I can see the effect on people and how people fall for it. It isn't that I never saw it . . . it is that I judged it. My Sister Marie would judge it: "Good girls don't do that." A beautiful woman is almost considered sinful . . . often scorned by women because of the effect they have on men.

And see . . . that just never fit with my mask of sympathetic understanding. In order to have everyone like me, be able to connect with everyone (which was a conscious goal as early as Gr. 9 for me), be able to go into everyone's world (the poor, the battered, the abused), I thought I had to forgo my physical beauty. Nail polish and fancy hair in the ghettos would never cut it.

Yet now, at 45, I find myself called to live out this other part of my life. It is like I have done my time being of service as a nun . . . and I am coming out.

The interesting thing is that I still have all my spiritual values and virtues and integrity. I still have a powerful mind. Now I get to have my body . . . and fun in my body. I let other people see and hear me. And I have quite fun doing it.

Along with healing came certain realizations that I wrote in my Morning Pages:

#1) I must change myself rather than the world.

#2) I must break my mask of sympathetic understanding. This one I am finding very interesting. As I live in my heart space . . . in my creative space, I repel all negativity.

I also had a new awareness of how many people often had to be involved in the creation, or enhancement, of beauty. When I was preparing my hair, nails, and costume for the performance, I couldn't help but remark on the sheer amount of energy that it took to produce physical beauty—to take care of hair, nails, face, feet, skin, and body. My hairstylist agreed vehemently. She said, "It takes a community."

Yes. There were so many people involved in the process of my "emergence." I had never really thought about it before then. There was my daughter, my class, my teachers, my clients, my students, hairstylists, makeup artists, wardrobe designers, and of course, all of my friends and the people who came to witness my journey. After the show, I wrote thank you notes to express my appreciation.

That night, watching my fellow students perform, I truly saw their talent and I enjoyed watching them shine. It made me joyful and it inspired me to see their final performances, knowing their struggles and having seen the birth process for each of them. I realized that night that I am part of a community. I realized that I may never again have such an intense experience getting to know other artists—intimately, really. We were in a unique situation—all growing together.

Being Seen by My Daughter

Just before my performance, I had the thought that I wanted to dedicate my story to Leila, my 11-year-old daughter. At the beginning, when I introduced my story, I said, "This is my story *Emerging*, which I wrote for my daughter Leila."

It was a complete surprise for Leila. She was delighted. One audience member said this was what touched her the most, to think about how this story was being passed on, how a daughter could witness her mother's act of courage. She was blown away to think about the impact that this must have on the daughter.

Another audience member told me that watching my daughter's reactions to my performance was by far the best part of the whole process. He thought that it was amazing.

This element of the process surprised me. It was something I never really planned. I only followed a little voice that told me to do it right before I performed. For it to have moved people so much astounds me. As a result, it will help me remember to trust those spontaneous, little voices.

Even before my performance, my participation in the program had begun to shift the way my daughter viewed me. Before I entered the program, she was quite unaware of what I really did and who I really was. She knew me as her mom, who was a therapist, yet confidentiality prevented me from sharing stories of my work, of what I really did. As an acting student, however, I could come home and share stories about my classes and the different students. Suddenly, before bedtimes, my daughter was asking me to tell her stories that happened in my classroom that day. I was enjoying telling her about my life. She was impressed with my new friends, my classmates, because she could really relate to them and she looked up to them.

The fact that she was keenly observing me and following the progress of the class became very clear on the drive home from the performance. I recorded the story in my Morning Pages:

> Leila said to me tonight, "Mom, I think you are in school to bring light to the class, to help them. I think you are like a Guardian Angel to everyone. I saw you help two people tonight."
>
> Leila has heard me wondering out loud, "What am I doing in school?" Her timing of her comment was impeccable. I had just finished telling her that I thought it was very sad that one of the student's Dad didn't show up. The student had written a story (and a song for the story) called "Lonely Girl." It was about her dad leaving her as a girl when her parents were divorced. The student had called him at 5 p.m. the day of the performance. The performance was at 7:30 p.m. He said he was working but that he'd be there. She knew he wouldn't be. He wasn't. In fact, I don't think anyone was there for her. Bummer.
>
> The reason Leila's timing was impeccable is that when I felt discouraged and disheartened and was in the kitchen at school crying, "Why am I here?" . . . it was this same

student, "Lonely Girl," who had said "Maybe you are here for others?"

I'll never forget that moment because I responded with, "Then I'm still being a therapist. That's what I always do . . . live my life for others."

So you see, Leila's timing . . . to say what she said just as I was talking about this same girl was like a sign to me to pay attention. Leila did not know that this student had told me the same thing. It was a synchronistic experience that helped me know that I might be in this school to help others.

I then asked Leila what she thought I was there to help them with. She said, "Learning that they can do it."

My Stage Name

Another development following the play was the creation of a new stage name for myself: "Duanita Gaye." "Luci Daye" was a pseudonym I had chosen to use as a stage name for the play. I had chosen the name carefully, had written it on all drafts of my scripts, and had been very clear with my instructor that I wanted to use this name for my performance. My reasoning was that a pseudonym would be easier because of the extreme difficulty in both pronouncing and spelling my given name, Duanita Eleniak.

Though everything had been planned for carefully, the Universe was to have none of it. When I arrived on the day of the performance, the programs all had me down as "Duanita Eleniak." I was introduced as such, with both my first and last names being terribly mispronounced, as has been the story of my life.

I took this as a message about the whole life test that I was moving through. One of my challenges was to be truly seen and heard, and the Universe ensured that I no longer hid behind any mask, by removing the final one I had tried on—that is, my desire to perform under a pseudonym. I was to put out my work as Duanita Eleniak, which took an infinitely greater amount of courage.

I was still concerned with mispronunciation of my name, however. I solved this by deciding to use my first and middle name as a stage name in the future—"Duanita Gaye." They were both my legal names, sounded good together and, because of the story about how I received them, I felt that they were truly the *essence* of me.

Duanita Gaye was the name given to me before I was born, by a teenager who lived in the Northern Alberta hamlet in which I grew up. This teenager babysat my older sister and was a close friend to my mother. One day, she told my mother (who was in her ninth month of pregnancy with me at that point) that Mom was going to have a girl and that she should name her Duanita Gaye. Very soon after, that teenager was killed along with many of the other teenagers in that small community when a train hit the high school bus. Several weeks later, on Christmas Day in 1960, I was born. I was a girl. I was Duanita Gaye.

Using "Duanita Gaye" as a stage name makes everything feel like I am finally being who I was meant to be in the world, doing what I was meant to do.

Overcoming Discouragement

I had been so discouraged so many times in the process of creating *Emerging*—when I was told that my peers (the teenagers) did not understand my words and, therefore, I needed to simplify my language; when my story was 25, then 15, then 12 minutes long, and I was continually asked to cut it; when no one in the class seemed to "get it," to get the deeper meaning and the implications for their own lives. All I could do at the time was to keep doing what I teach others to do. I kept applying the principles I was learning in quantum physics, and I constantly refused to think the discouraging thoughts that kept floating through my mind. I knew they would do me no good—in fact, they could suck me into the quicksand of quitting.

I just kept going with the invention of myself as an artist; developing the characters in the story; developing the atmospheres in the story; taking care of props (wardrobe, masks); and attending to details like arranging appointments (hair, makeup, skin, dress fittings). Reflecting back on it now, I can see that I just kept on taking small creative actions every day—

right up to the moment before the performance, the most creative actions being the choice of which thoughts I would allow myself to think.

I had moved through my own lack of courage, through the many times I felt discouraged. I just never allowed myself to think about it—or my fear. I never denied my fear and my feelings of discouragement. They were there, popping into my mind and body with regular frequency. I just never stopped to focus on them. OK. I lie. I did allow myself to think about it on at least two occasions; however, these were horrible experiences. I ended up crying, going deeper and deeper into helplessness and hopelessness, questioning what I was doing there, and so on . . .

On those occasions, what got me through was community. During my meltdown in the school kitchen, two fellow students responded to my cry of "What am I doing here?" with "Well, maybe you're here for others." Even though the comment made me angry at the time, it served to give me the larger perspective that I so greatly needed.

My teacher had also come into the kitchen. Now, he never comes into the kitchen, yet he came in that day and he sat very quietly. I knew that he was there because he saw my struggle and he wanted to help. I also knew that he knew, and I knew, that he did not know how to help me at the time. When I asked him if he "got" my story, he replied with, "No. I honestly have to say that I don't." This was one of my major discouragements. No one seemed to be getting it. I questioned my ability to communicate effectively. Though I would find myself as a writer vibrating with excitement at the computer with each rewrite, my conviction about the brilliance of the work did not seem to be coming across to the audience.

Though he knew that these were words I did not want to hear, he said them. He spoke his truth—and I love him for that. And it did pay off in the end, because simplifying the story did make it more understandable, effective, and powerful. What amazed me was that though his words only amplified my feelings of discouragement, his mere presence there in the kitchen—his willingness to be there, to witness my pain, to feel helpless along with me, to support me in my process—this is what helped me feel encouraged. He wanted to help me and I could feel his pain at being unable to do anything except be there. The ironic thing is that it was his willingness to be there that was what counted at that moment. The rest was up to me.

The third thing that moved me past the block of discouragement was watching carefully for signs and holding faith in the images themselves. For example, the very day when I did my first reading in class and when I felt most discouraged (because I had to change my language, simplify, cut, and no one was getting it anyway), one student responded to my reading with a painting. She said that my story had inspired an idea for a painting of a butterfly for her, something that doesn't happen very often. She thanked me for inspiring her.

This was a sign, a synchronicity. I had been holding the intention that my story inspires others to develop and act on their creativity, to live their dream—and here was someone (who did not know my intentions) who had been inspired. This synchronicity was a sign that gave me the courage to hold my faith in the images and the truth—and to keep going.

Neurological Changes

Immediately after the play was over, my heart began beating and I had a headache. It was an unusual headache because it was mostly a really strong muscle ache radiating from the base of my skull on my left side. I also was seeing lights, doughnut—shaped circles of lights in front of my eyes made up of tiny triangles of light. I attempted to blink them away to no avail. I thought I would get a migraine and debated even taking an aspirin the next day, because I had to work. I loaded up on water instead and the pain moved through. The intensely sore shoulders and neck remained even four days later.

Because one of the lessons I learned in my story was to view my body as a tool, I looked up my symptoms on Louise Hay's list of correlations between diseases and probable negative thought-pattern causes. I wanted to explore possible emotional and thought connections that I might make to ease the pain. My research unearthed the following affirmations with which I began to work:

Neck: I am flexible. I welcome other viewpoints.

Head: Peace, love, joy, relaxation. I relax into the flow of life and let life flow through me with ease.

59

Shoulders: I release anger in harmless ways. Life is joyous and free. All that I accept is good.

Knee: Forgiveness, tolerance, compassion. I move forward without hesitation.

Liver: I let go of everything that I no longer need. My consciousness is now cleansed and my concepts are fresh, new, and vital.

Eyes: I am free. I look ahead freely because life is eternal and filled with joy. I see with loving eyes. No one can ever hurt me.

Heart: Joy, love, peace. I joyfully accept life.

It was also about this time, four days after the performance, that I began noticing neurological changes in myself. I had been working diligently for the whole time leading up to the performance to re-create myself as an artist. My aim was to do so by physically altering my neuronets—that is, the intricate nets of neurons that come together to form thought patterns. When I first noticed the neurological changes in myself, I joked about it in my Morning Pages, thinking the condition would be temporary and was most likely there because I was tired:

I think I have become an artist. My gas tank was almost empty today; my house and car are a mess; and I couldn't remember if I had got the children's birthday presents.

Now, this just isn't like me. It is, however, certainly like a lot of artists I know. What about my responsibilities and obligations?

I remembered the words in *What the Bleep Do We Know!?* (2004): "How do you know if you have shifted consciousness? Look around you and see if anything has changed." I was seeing changes in my external environment and I could relate them directly to new ways that I could see myself processing information. Some of the ways felt wonderful, like seeing color, lights, and shapes more sharply; feeling more relaxed; and understanding situations with more flexibility.

Other changes I began to notice were a bit scary. For example, I used to type a minimum 100 words per minute with no errors. After the performance, my fingers refused to go down on the keyboard in the same automatic way. What I was thinking and what I was typing were two different things. I would go back to my mistakes and consciously focus on bringing my thoughts down to the keyboard through my fingertips, often to no avail. The connection between my thoughts and my fingers' memory of the keyboard seemed to be interfered with.

I also noticed information retrieval problems. Before the performance I could easily recall names of people, books, etcetera, especially those that I worked with a lot. After the performance I would often have memory lapses. I would know exactly what I wanted to retrieve and I would know that I knew the information, yet I would be unable to access it. Often the material would pop up on its own accord way after the time I was working on remembering it. I also noticed changes in my speech. Frequently I would catch myself switching word order around inappropriately in a sentence.

These changes were so pronounced that initially they fascinated me. Had I actually succeeded in shifting my neuronets around? Or had I just had a slight stroke that evening? Or both? If I actually had shifted my neuronets around, the power of intentions became very apparent to me. I would never again be so casual about encouraging people to use intentions, because one might never be able to predict the side effects. This experience underscored the importance of being careful what you ask for.

Initially, I decided to monitor when and how these changes surfaced and what the benefit of the changes might be to a person who has created a reality of being an artist. There were changes in my behavior. For example, I would more often stay quiet now, rather than speak out, for fear of scrambling my words or failing to remember something and sounding like a fool. This gave me an opportunity to listen to people more, to observe them more—and to observe my own reactions to people.

I also began to have more empathy and understanding for people who have special needs when it comes to learning, processing, and retrieving information. I began to realize how blessed I had been to have been quick with accessing and processing information. It was one of those gifts that I did not appreciate when I had it, because I had never known what it was to be without it.

When the symptoms remained, I settled into an acceptance of my new state of being—pleased in some way that something physical had happened that night of the performance, which no one could dispute. I knew that even on a body level I had gone through substantial changes. My symptoms were my evidence.

Then suddenly, one day, I realized how silly I was to be holding on to these concrete symptoms and to be settling into an "acceptance" of them in my life. After all, if I was honest, sometimes it just downright annoying to have these processing issues. Typing could now be a frustrating and time-consuming process. Whereas I never had to proof my work before, slowing down and proofing was now a necessity. One day I was listening to Dr. Joe Dispenza's (2005) lecture on how people rebuild neuronets using imagination and intention, which allows them to bring limbs back to function after things like accidents and strokes. Suddenly I realized that maybe the lesson in these symptoms was for me to learn how to reverse them and regain my full functioning, rather than accept my decline in functioning.

Since that realization I have been working to regain my capacities. The neurological symptoms persist, although they have declined in frequency and intensity. My mistakes typing, for example, are fewer and I am usually able to consciously make my fingers type corrections. My speech lapses are less frequent as well.

The symptoms are still strong enough to change my behavior. I am still quieter than I used to be. I have a much more increased tolerance level for mess and chaos. I prefer to write with a pen rather than type. Even if it is a slower process, the former is a far less frustrating way to put my thoughts into words. And I still wonder about the good in the changes that happened. For example, maybe this work was meant to be written by hand first. Maybe it was meant to be cooked up slowly, in a quiet room without the light of the computer on my face or the hum in my ears. Maybe the words and the whole spirit of my story changes when it slides onto ruled paper through a favorite pen. Maybe.

Other Changes, Intriguing Questions

Apart from neurological changes, my daughter pointed out a change in my general mood, which is reflected in this story I wrote in my Morning Pages:

> Yesterday Leila got a C+. She is usually an A student. She forgot titles in her graph . . . stuff like that . . . silly stuff. I was upset yet I kept remembering all the stuff I have been forgetting over the past week and I realized that it happens to all of us and we just have to keep going. In the end, it really makes no difference at all. So then she says, "Mommy, you used to get angry with me . . . now you aren't."

The process and performance of *Emerging* seemed to have left me with more questions than answers. For example, how could I know for sure if anything had really changed? Leila seemed to think so. She confirmed a perception of mine that a lot of my angry energy had dissipated, that my responses to her and others had changed.

I kept wondering how I would know when and if my neuronets had changed, when and if my intentions would be brought into reality. Part of me felt like a child saying continually, "Are we there yet?"

When I looked around me, I could see that my life circumstances were changing. For example, I had moved into a new studio for my art therapy practice. Synchronistically, the District refused to give me a business license as a therapist but would give me a license as an artist. I recognized this as a possible sign that the world was now seeing me as an artist. Maybe my intentions to emerge as one were met?

I began to wonder things like: when old neuronets dissolve and new ones are formed, is there a toxic waste release that might feel like muscles that were worked to the point of exhaustion? Are there physical symptoms that go along with running at higher frequencies? What are they? I wondered in my Morning Pages:

> Did my work on *Emerging* shift people to a new level of consciousness? A new paradigm? How would I know that? How can I know this for sure? I guess, more importantly,

did my work shift me to a new level of consciousness? To be reborn as an artist . . . what does that mean? How do I know when my attitudes shift? How do I know when my reality changes? In the movie they say—look around you . . . have things changed? What is the ripple effect of me showing these people what I am going through?

In response to my question, "How will I know what kind of ripple effect my performance caused for others?" I wrote in my Morning Pages:

> Little signs: Leila began spontaneously humming "We All Come from the Mother" the day after the concert. One of the students over the rest of the year would also begin to sing this chant. Somehow, it had sunk into their awareness and memories.
>
> Several times throughout the year students would tease each other by calling each other "Sister Marie" if they caught each other being "self-critical." The first time I overheard this, I was shocked. I realized that not only had my story been understood, it had been integrated in these young people's experience, and remembered.

Through the process of creating and completing my first performance project, I realized that people love true stories, that truth in and of itself adds vitality. What is interesting about this project is that I began with the intention of moving people to a new state of consciousness through the arts. Then I realized that I needed simply to do this for myself. I realized I could identify the change (feel it, learn about it), create experiences where the change is there, and repeat this process until it is in my being.

One of the best things about *Emerging*—my first test as a performing artist—was my discovery that an actress is a storyteller and that I love the storyteller's journey. That I know for sure. It is a truly healing journey. One must travel it to know it. You never know what you will encounter on the way or where it will lead you. The magic often comes on the night when it is actually performed with an audience. The alchemy happens when it is performed. The transformation occurs.

I emerged as a woman more solid in her ability to be seen and heard, to appreciate her body, and to stay grounded in her power.

six

Mother Teresa and Billie's Shoes

Second Test: The Play—*Balm in Gilead*

After the first six months of working intensely with my class, it was time to move into the second semester and begin the next major test: preparation for the performance of a play—and a powerful lesson about oneness and community.

During the first semester of courses, my classmates and I had shared some of our deepest stories as we worked to access particular emotions for scripts—stories that made us cry, that made us angry, and that made us sexual. We shared our wants, our dreams, our hopes, and our fears. I thought that we knew each other very well and I felt very close to them. Many of them considered me to be a mother figure because of the age difference between us.

In January, as the new semester began, I was seriously considering offering my classmates one of my courses in self-esteem and self-empowerment, because it had become clear to me how building these two factors could be really useful to them. I wanted to help them all, in whatever way I could, to be the very best that they could be. I could see how fear and emotional blocks were getting in the way of their work as actors. I actually designed a whole course according to what I could see they would need, set out a timeline, and considered how such a course might weave into my PhD research. In hindsight, I can recognize that I was still at a place of wanting to fix others, rather than simply being "the change that I wanted to see in the world."

As I pondered the possibility of offering my fellow students a course, several things happened that made me quickly reconsider and question the wisdom of such an endeavor. I would be in an unusual position—that is, I would be in a multiple role of researcher/ fellow student/teacher. The more the play progressed, the more I came to see my classmates' different sides, and the more the idea of doing a course for them dissipated—as did my connection to them.

The Unwritten Play

The purpose of doing a play was to give us an experience of performing for theater, which is a very different form than film and television. It would also provide an experience of working in community.

It had been a very long time since I had been really involved in a group project without being the leader of the group. Working in groups as a peer has always been an incredibly frustrating experience for me. In my life, I usually choose to work alone or with a highly select group of handpicked people. For this project, however, I was simply a group member, one of a group of eleven classmates (most of whom were 20 to 26 years my junior). I began in great excitement and anticipation, which quickly subsided as I succumbed to the collective decisions of the group, and as a place in the community was whittled out of me.

During the initial phases of the theater project, our teacher gave us choices, one of which could be to write our own play. I really wanted to break off with a small group of classmates and write a play. Over the Christmas break, I had become intrigued with the question, "What is a 21st-century play?" inspired by a contest I had checked out. I wanted to write a "21st-century play," dealing with content based on the principles of quantum physics. I wanted to sink into a meaningful project that could give the audience a transformational experience. I wanted to try out new material in an intentional way, to alter the audience's consciousness.

Well, none of my high expectations were to come to pass. The class could not reach a consensus whether to write one play, form groups and write many plays, or do a play that was already written. Finally, the teacher simply chose a play for us and assigned us the characters. We were to do *Balm in Gilead*, by Lanford Wilson.

I was devastated. My image of writing a play and weaving in what I was learning about the way the universe worked was shattered. We were going to do the play *Balm in Gilead*, a play about drug addicts, prostitutes, thieves, and junkies in a café. Since the play was written for 32 characters and we were a cast of 12, I was to be a character that combined three of the parts: the restaurant owner, the guy who ran the restaurant, and the waitress. I eventually called her "Billie."

The Dream That Connected Me

Initially I was overwhelmed with the disappointment at having to do a written play rather than write one. The worse thing was that this play required immersion in feelings like anger, depression, and grief—which calibrate very low on the Map of Consciousness, and which were so opposite to the feelings that I wanted to bring to the world through my art. I was also uncomfortable with the need to create one character out of three. I could find no point of connection to the play and was upset about having to invest time and energy doing it. Initially, the only thing that kept me from giving up (and getting really negative) was the instructor, who has an amazing talent to encourage and inspire despite all the odds.

Then it happened. I had a dream:

> *A man wanted me to run a restaurant. At first, I thought this was a ridiculous idea and then I remembered my husband, that this was his dream. He loved coffee, was excellent at making coffee, and had excellent skills in talking and connecting with people, something that he loved to do. I could see him running a coffee shop, no problem.*

I had this dream just after being told what the play, and my role in it, was going to be. The dream lifted the thick cloak of disappointment, sadness, negativity, and resistance into which I had fallen, because it was a synchronistic event. My inner world was meeting my outer world and I was being given a point of entry into the play, into my character. It was a gift of connection to the task set before me.

A great gift this was indeed, for not only did it lift the darkness and allow me into the material, but it also gave me a purpose for doing the play at another level. At the dream level, I was being called or invited to run this coffee shop not because it met my needs or desires, but because I was to agree to do it out of the love and understanding I had for my "husband." In some ways it was a sacrifice of my own needs and desires in order to assist my "husband" to actualize his passions and create an environment where all of his skills and talents could shine brightly.

The dream helped me have a deep knowing that this play was being done for a higher purpose, with the ultimate motivation of "love" behind it. This knowing assisted both me and others in the cast as we trudged through the thick, heavy energy that was to unfold during production.

Fueled and lifted by the dream that I now call "Coffee House Husband," I set out my intentions for the play—see **Creative Inspiration VI**. My connection to and creation of my character came easily and quickly. I began by imagining Billie's history, which I wrote as a monologue:

> I am Billie. I work at the café because it was my late husband's dream to do so. I had ended up on the street at 15 years old, where I met my husband, who, at the time, was a drug dealer and a pimp. I had been prostituting myself to survive but when we met, something happened. Real love happened and my husband wanted a different life for us. So, he got us work in a café in that area of town, just serving coffee. But we knew the crowd and accepted them, having been one of them.
>
> Eventually we wanted to own our own place, with even the white picket fence. That's the thing about my husband, he was a dreamer and he took the steps needed to get there. And with the love we had, we were actually doing it, you know. We were both clean, sober, and off the streets.
>
> But then I got pregnant . . . which was great and we were so happy. But then there were lots of problems with the pregnancy, you know? And my husband wanted the best medical help possible for me. So, I didn't know it at the time, but he got back into selling drugs to pay the

medical bills for me and the baby. And, of course, he didn't give the money back to the main dealer . . . he used it for the bills instead.

So . . . they shot him. Right there in the coffee shop. Right there when we were both working a shift. They shot him. And the baby . . . well, she died anyhow. Too small.

So . . . I stayed there and kept working just like my husband had dreamed we would.

Mother Teresa and Billie

I loved bringing Billie to life because I found that she had a life of her very own. Though I had developed characters before as a writer for novels and screenplays, I had never before developed a character as an actor. The big difference, I discovered, was that I actually had to "be" this character. I had to change myself physically, emotionally, and intellectually in order to allow her to come through me in a very real way.

For the most part, this was easy because I found so many ways in which Billie and I are the same. For example, in the play, Billie is constantly working. Before the play begins, she is up and prepping the food for the restaurant. After the play ends, she goes home and preps for the next day before going to sleep. She is a woman who is on her feet working hard from the time she gets up to the time she goes to sleep . . . serving, constantly serving others. "I love Billie"—I wrote in my Morning Pages—"I really love Billie":

> I really am Billie. I can relate to being a hard-working woman who makes an honest living . . . She is actually a totally wonderful character. Mother-Teresa-like. Billie prays, "Mother Teresa . . . I am dealing with bums. Help me to be patient. Help me to be kind. Help me to be loving to them, as if they are my own children."

As soon as the connection to Mother Teresa came up, I realized that, indeed, faith was what kept Billie going every day through all the heaviness of her life. Once again, this was a profound connection to my own character, for it is my faith that helps to move me through difficult times. Here is one of Billie's prayers that I recorded in my Morning Pages:

> Bird Woman Billie's Prayer: Great Creator. I suffer so much. I hate my reality. I hate all the work—the hard work—my body aches and each day I clean and cook and I have to take care of everything . . . and I just want to be a good woman. Help me to be like Mother Teresa. Help me to be grateful for each of these people in the restaurant—each day . . . with each thing they ask me to do. Mother Teresa, help me to have your patience and your compassion. Help me to provide a place of shelter for them . . . help me to help them. Help me to stop being angry with them . . . and angry with their attitudes . . . So anyway, God. Let's create a day . . . and I know just what to say and do. And God . . . take good care of my Joe . . . and help me to know that he sees me working at the little coffee shop—just like was his dream.

And as I prayed as Billie, I struggled with my own demons:

> And for me . . . I feel I am suffering with this play. Yesterday I was impatient, scared, blaming, judging . . . yet I cannot do any of that because I myself am still waiting to be totally off book. I can see community happening. We need each other in a very sick kind of way . . . we are all joined together.
>
> And for me . . . well . . . this isn't the reality I want or live or even show to the world . . . the misery, the suffering. When I think of transformational theater, I think of helping people to feel love, joy, peace, bliss. Shifting the emotional experience there in order to bring that to reality.
>
> Why would I even want to show this pain, suffering, misery? Why would I want to feel it as an actor? To

connect to it enough that the audience feels it? Why is it important for the world to see?

As a new social worker 25 years ago, I would have been right in there, helping people . . . giving food, clean needles, blankets . . . ensuring that their plight was noticed. Yet now I find myself hardened somewhat to the plight. I know the message in the play, that is, that these people are like cockroaches. They survive. And you find them in century after century . . . as far as you can dig back in time. And they'll be there in the future too.

I guess I have become disillusioned because in my naiveté as a new social worker, I was looking for a "cure" for poverty. And, the older I get, the more I realize that these people are there as an opportunity for us to learn to love people for who they are; to learn to refrain from judgment; to give without expecting anything back.

Initially the teacher said that we do this play to give a voice to these people. I challenged him. "And say what?" I asked. He looked at me. My negativity and cynicism popped his bubble. Then, interestingly, just as we moved into doing this play, in my private practice I moved into working with a woman who was on the streets and then was scared straight. She now works with hookers to help them off the streets. She said she was asked to talk to some reporters and she thought to herself, "And what are they doing about this? They report on it and then they go home with their fancy camera equipment. Yet there are so many people who need love out there."

Yet there are so many people who need love out there—that really got me. *What am I doing? I am doing a play about the reality of their lives and I am giving them love . . . unconditional love for a moment of truthfulness in an imaginary circumstance. Yet our brain doesn't care if it is real or imagined.*

I began to call directly on the same spirit I was working with in my daily affirmations about my PhD project, to assist me in my work on the play, as my "Co-Create My Day" entry in my Morning Pages indicates:

> Team Spirit, today we put everything we've got into focusing and concentrating on the play, on my character . . . on my relationship to the other characters. Today I have an experience of being Billie and I create an atmosphere of warmth and *home* in the theater. I pray. I remember my dead husband. I catch many things on many levels. People love working with me and I just shine. My character just shines. I know all of my lines. I am able to get into the actions. And, most importantly, you are with me, guiding me continually to Billie—to being there in truth. And you show me in an unexpected way that leaves me no doubt that we've hit it. And what we do makes it best for everyone. All is well in our world.

I began to weave all aspects of my life into the development of Billie. For example, in the voice class I was taking, I asked to sing the song "Feed the Birds," by Larson & Larson. The song is sung by a bag woman begging on the street corner in the Disney movie *Mary Poppins*. When I connected a song to my character, several beautiful dimensions opened up for me. As a singer, the character development I was doing provided a richness and depth to the feeling and emotion of the lyrics. This connection of song to character resulted in my performing the song "Feed the Birds" in the character of Billie at a parent performance night at my daughter's school.

The song also opened up another dimension to Billie's character. I realized that she saves the breadcrumbs and scraps of bread from the café and bags them when she gets home in order to sell them to people so that they could feed the birds. This particular imagination became very important during the play, because it gave me purpose and intent behind some of the "work" of the character during the play. When I cleaned up after the other characters in the cast I would bag the bread, knowing that I would be taking it to sell on the corner so that birds could be fed and I could make a little more money toward the dream of the white picket-fenced home that my late husband and I had imagined together.

As Duanita, I began taking bread out to feed the birds during my morning walks. I practiced walking as a woman who was on her feet every day. I bought special shoes at a Value Village that were what a hard-working waitress would wear. They squeaked and creaked, which helped me remember how sore Billie's bones were. They made me move from side to side and stand with my legs apart. I began taking morning walks in Billie's shoes and rehearsed inner monologues to allow for connection to the character.

As easy in some ways as it was to connect with Billie's character, it was also just as difficult. Physically I stopped taking care of my hair, nails, face, and feet before the performance, in order to get a truly physically ragged look. My face felt dry, my hair felt wiry, my gray roots were showing, my nails were ragged, and my hands dry. Looking like this, particularly after having been sensitized to the impact of aesthetics, was a very humbling experience. All of my original intentions to morph into an actress that looked like Sophia Loren, Audrey Hepburn, and Shirley MacLaine seemed very far away. Instead of becoming "classically beautiful" as I had set in my original intentions, I was now morphing into a bag lady.

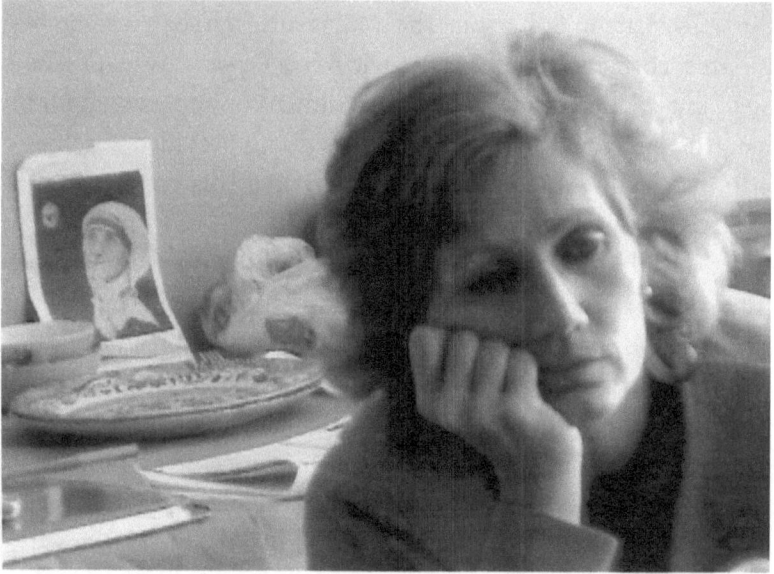

Image of Billie, played by Duanita Gaye, in *Balm in Gilead*, by Lanford Wilson; photograph by Philip Granger

Blurring of Art and Life

My greatest challenge was moving into and staying in the consciousness field of Billie, a character that lives mostly at the level of despair. As always, my Morning Pages mirrored what I was experiencing:

> As Billie I hate . . . I hate my life, I hate myself. I pray to make it better. People bother me. I am quite fed up with people coming into my space or going into the till. And I put up my boundaries. I don't care what they think of me. And I really hate when they put real decent work down. Sometimes I am resentful that I do all the work. I work hard . . . I do the decent living . . . then other people want to sponge off of me. And I feel this. I really do feel this. I see it happening in the dynamics of the cast. I have moved through some of my blocks by keeping at it on a daily basis. And, you know, I find myself hating her [a fellow actress] for coming in and wriggling her ass at the teacher. And the men. I see the men like "bees to honey" . . . they come in droves to her. And I am unnoticed. Here I am in my little world, like Billie.

As my writing indicates, during the weeks of rehearsals, the line between me—Duanita—and Billie became very blurred. The more I sunk into the character of Billie, the more I became sadder, depressed, despairing, angry, and negative. The relationships between Billie and the other characters in the play began to spill over into "real" life. First and foremost, I simply did not trust any of them. This feeling was the same whether I was Billie and they were in their roles as pimps, whores, liars, and thieves, or when I was Duanita and they were my fellow classmates and actors. On a consistent basis, my peers missed rehearsals, and/or came late, and/or came unprepared. The play is written in a way that is extremely interdependent, each person cuing off another's words. It is a play where professionalism and preparation is even more important than usual. In order to cope with my role, which threaded in and through all sections, I audiotaped rehearsals and would practice my cues and lines in the car on the way to and from school (40 minutes per day), in order to assist the memorization process.

To deal with cast members not being there and being unprepared and missing cues during rehearsals, I just became Billie and prayed. I would literally sit praying in rehearsals, at the very end of my rope of patience, feeling like I was about to explode as I watched more precious rehearsal time being eaten up, with the director giving yet another lecture on taking responsibility as an actor, on remembering that the other cast members were relying on everyone else, and that the work needed to be done so that we could trust each other on stage. I felt sorry for him.

I made the choice to use the anger and disillusionment and despair I was feeling in my role as Billie. I sat through rehearsals feeling upset, angry, and depressed and told people who expressed concern that I was just getting into my character—which was true to some extent. I had to learn how to work with this group of students and remember to apply the principles of quantum physics that I was learning—I had to accept full responsibility for what was happening, to remember that we are all "one," and to espouse compassion, kindness, a non-judgemental attitude, and positive thinking. It was like walking through fire just to see if I could remain positive and keep my connection with joy, love, and peace.

I was aware of the weight of negativity pulling me down and had to learn to lift myself. I discovered that one of the best ways to snap out of the foul mood I fell into during rehearsals was to get in my car and put on some happy music. Initially I would just let the music wash over me while I cried or raged. But then I discovered that singing along was the quickest and surest "snap" back to the place I usually lived my life—that is, feeling joy and love a fair majority of my waking hours. I also discovered that I just had to let go. I stopped caring about whether we performed the play or not, whether it was good or not. I simply stayed with what I had control over, my character and her performance, and I decided to just remain grateful for what I could.

"I am grateful for this play," I wrote in my Morning Pages. "I am grateful to recognize that the grief and sadness and anger/ annoyance I feel is Billie's . . . that I am so connected to the character . . . that I become the character." I also continued to work with such intentions as: "I am an award-winning actress. People believe me because I become the role."

Despite the lack of preparation, two performance dates were set; the DVD mentioned above has a recording of the opening night. The day before the performance, the director worked day and night, almost alone, to create the set. The result was a magnificent set that brought the whole coffee shop alive with atmosphere. What could have been the only complete full dress rehearsal on that day was a piecemeal one at best, due to actors not showing. When some of the key actors that were there made it obvious that they still had not memorized their lines, the director confronted them.

For weeks I had watched him attempt to persuade, cajole, shame, and convince the cast to learn their lines, to come to rehearsals, to be on time—all to no avail. Here it was, the night before the performance and a dress rehearsal could not happen. The end result was that we were to move to performance without even one full dress rehearsal and with many unprepared actors.

Opening Night

On opening night I was afraid. One of the ways that I prepare myself for a role is repetition. In an ideal world, I would have loved to run the whole play with full cast several times before performing it. I discovered that preparation of this kind helps me feel safe as an actor. Yet, on opening night, this was not the situation at all.

I came early before the performance, as per the director's instructions, to find that only some cast members were there. I went into makeup where they helped me look even more tired, depressed, and sad. My fellow classmates were in there as well, getting "track marks" and black eyes and bruises.

Just before the performance I blocked out the entire play on Billie's order pad so that I could refer to it if necessary. Bottom line was that I felt unprepared. Though I had run my lines thousands of times with the audiotapes I made during rehearsals, I had done that on my own. I could not trust my fellow actors to cue me with their lines. So, in order to feel safe, I took in the pad with the blocking of the play. It helped me feel like I could deal with anything that would happen.

Just before we went on, the dynamics in the green room among the actors were awful. Several were totally angry with each other because they came late. Some were still totally angry with the director. We all knew that there were directors, casting agents, and agents in the audience, and nerves were running high.

Despite all this, just before we went on, we all sang a song that had been taught in our voice class. It was an African tribal song. Somehow this song brought back our connection as a class and the good feelings that we had also experienced for one another through this intense immersion in the entire program. The song gave us a feeling of strength and togetherness before we moved onstage.

And then we were onstage. It was the first time I was fully working as Billie in the café. The venue was small—so small, in fact, that the front row of the audience was about two feet from the front of my counter, and audience members sat right beside and behind me in my "kitchen"! We were playing to a full house. It was extremely hot in the room. The heat, the size of the room, and the lack of preparedness of the cast all contributed to creating an extremely intense atmosphere.

If nothing else, at least the set design was holding its own. The director had succeeded, almost single-handedly, in creating a believable skid row "café" with a doorway, so that some of the action could be played on the "street." He had brought wallpaper and table covers and art and fabric with which he had literally transformed the space. To this he added creative lighting and music, which was a final touch that generated truth, believability, and realism.

Over my years as an art therapist, I have become very aware of space and creating space. I have learned how trust, respect, and an atmosphere of openness can easily be created in a therapy space and felt by clients without saying or doing anything. It was amazing to experience this as I walked onto the set for the first time on opening night as Billie. I could literally feel what the director had made while creating the space. The "something" that I was feeling was what Chekov (1985) identified as "atmosphere." The director had spent time in the room while creating the set, imagining an atmosphere of relative safety for street people within the confines of their local café. Using line, shape, color, and objects, he created a café that was warm and homey and had a sense of safety, despite the storm in which the characters lived.

As I walked onto the set in full costume, I felt Billie come alive in me. It was like I simply took a backseat to her. She loved her café and it was easy for her to take loving care of it. As a result, it was easy for me to create and do the "work" of Billie during the play. With love and genuine caring for the café, I swept the floor, wiped the tables, emptied ashtrays, did the dishes, and carried the food. I had been worried about actually working with real food since opening night would be the first time I did it in that space. But I had rehearsed it so thoroughly in my mind, thinking through each detail (for instance, knives necessary, garbage bags for the garbage can, water containers) that the props fell smoothly into place that night.

Doing the "work" of Billie helped me "drop" into place in my body in order to become her. I felt my feet ache, my back ache, the stiffness of Billie's body as I never had previously. It was as if someone else was walking in my body. I was also able to "drop" very easily into Billie's consciousness. I felt down, defeated, a bit numb, and beaten by the world. I felt irritable, loving, kind, angry, and a whole range of other emotions as I interacted with the other characters. So intensely did I move into this physical and psychological state that I became unaware of the audience. I was Billie, working in my café as I had done day in and day out for years and years.

Another part of me, Duanita, was never able to let go, however. This part of me stayed ready, on guard during the entire performance, alert to ensuring that the play would be done well. I regretted that this part of me had to be so alert and conscious during the performance, although it did prove necessary. Actors blew lines continually, making it difficult to follow and to know when to cue in. Some of the lines were cues to me; others were cues between other actors. As a result, there were what our director described as "holes big enough to drive a huge truck through" in our play.

To the audience it may just have seemed like a slow pace was being set. To the alert part of me it was a frantic inner monologue time of "Where are we? Who blew that? What needs to be said now? How can I cover? Who covered? How can I weave my part in now?" On two occasions, I did have to refer to the blocking that I had written earlier on Billie's pad on, just to reorient to where we were and where we needed to go in the flow. The biggest challenge on opening night happened in Act II when one actor literally missed his entrance and we were all scrambling to keep the play moving.

I really enjoyed the experience of being Billie in her café—I enjoyed feeling the physical and psychological reality. However, I felt no degree of success or joy or happiness after the play was over. I just felt relief. I was relieved that I no longer had to live in Billie's consciousness. I was relieved that I no longer had to work with that cast, as it was an exercise in frustration, and I found myself leaving the stage wanting to avoid the anger, the letdown, the disappointment, the disbelief, and the mistrust that I was indeed feeling toward fellow cast members.

I walked away from the play after closing night early, collecting my props and leaving the cast to party. I did not feel like partying. I felt like crying. I felt like being alone. I did not even want to think about the experience and, indeed, am only writing about it now, six months after completion. I was grateful that the closing of the play was the beginning of semester break. I went for a facial, manicure, pedicure, haircut, and color; and I took care of my body again. I had stopped all of this in preparation for the role of Billie. I rested. I put the play out of my mind. I never wanted to think of it again. Because all of the good stuff that happened for me through this intense experience was overshadowed by such heavy feelings of negativity, I just needed to pull out and feel like myself again.

Billie's Shoes

Just before opening night I had been dismayed to find that my car had been broken into in the parking lot. Besides some change, the thieves only stole one thing—Billie's shoes.

The parking lot is in the downtown core of Vancouver, near Hastings Street, an area very much akin to the type of area where Billie's café would have been in New York (well, the Canadian version of a "rough area" of New York). In fact, as part of our research for the play, as a class we walked Hastings in order to watch and get ideas for our characters. On our walk we observed people who were pimping, prostituting, selling drugs, and taking drugs. We even had coffee in a small café in the area, the same café where our teacher had found someone dead in the washroom during his last class field visit.

It was in this Hastings café, through observing the two waitresses, that I came up with the idea of worn-down running shoes for Billie. Up to that point we had also been playing with the idea of slippers or nursing uniform-type shoes. I had loved the runners that I found at a second-hand shop. They were worn in and dirty. Most importantly, however, they creaked and groaned. They talked when I walked. Because of the way they were worn in, they made me walk shifting my weight from side to side, more like a waddle and a shuffle than a walk.

Those shoes were really Billie's. They made my character. They helped me remember how sore my feet and bones were when I became Billie. They helped me remember to lower the center in my body when I became Billie. Those shoes had character, and now, one day before opening night, they were gone—stolen. I was in shock. The irony and synchronicity of the situation overwhelmed me. Who would steal a pair of such broken-down old shoes, except someone who was obviously living the reality of the life to which the character Billie belonged. Billie's shoes had gone to live in the reality of street life on Hastings Street in Vancouver. They had crossed over from the truth and reality of Billie's world in my imagination to the outer world of crime, drugs, and pathos.

I couldn't help but wonder where the shoes went, those shoes that I had charged with so much intention. Who was walking in Billie's shoes now? Who was hearing them creak and groan and talk of the pain and suffering of a life filled with hard work and heartache? Who was feeling Billie's prayers ripple from the shoes into the very soles of their feet, prayers that would carry them through the desperation just as they did Billie?

To this day I still look for Billie's shoes on the feet of the people on Hastings.

Faced with the shock of Billie's shoes being stolen by a street person, and with no time to replace them, I was overwhelmed when my director generously offered to find some shoes for Billie. I knew that he had made the offer because he could see how powerfully the incident had affected me. His powers of observation often amazed me.

For example, when I realized that the way Billie survived was to pray and I recognized the connection between Billie and Mother Teresa—both serving "the poorest of the poor"—I brought a picture of Mother Teresa to the set. I taped it to the wall in Billie's kitchen area just above where I stood as her, washing dishes. This praying was a very private part of Billie—and a deeply private part of me. During rehearsals, when I would see the image of Mother Teresa, I would remember to pray and I would pray as Billie for all the lost souls I was serving in the café. Simultaneously, I would pray as Duanita for all the lost, struggling souls in my class, unable to commit fully to the work. None of my classmates asked about the image of Mother Teresa that went up on the wall every rehearsal. The director, however, noticed it immediately.

Though he was always so busy with a million and one details related to the rehearsals, he stopped when he saw it and looked at me. At first I thought he was going to question my choice, and I found myself really attached to the image and steeling myself for questions. Instead, I felt his knowing look pierce me and, with no real words spoken, I knew that he understood what I was doing with the image and how it connected. In that moment I had a deep feeling of being understood as an artist. It was like finding a soul mate where words were unnecessary, and the wild and weird places to which my artistic mind leaps were all just understood.

It was this same sense of understanding that pervaded the atmosphere when he heard that Billie's shoes were stolen. He knew how significant this was and wanted to make it better for me. Though I was grateful for his offer to get me new shoes, I really did not expect that he would ever remember such a detail with everything else that was going on. I saw him single-handedly preparing the details of the set, calming down young actors falling apart with nerves, running around, and prepping details (like framing images of the poster for the play for each cast member and getting bracelets for us as gifts. My bracelet said "Freedom"). I could see how overwhelming his world was; I thanked him for his generous offer and set about finding myself shoes.

As I headed off on my errand, a part of me was watching to see if he would actually remember his offer. Several hours before I needed to be at the school for opening night, I received a call from the school secretary, informing me that the director wanted me to know that he had been unable to find me shoes for Billie. I thanked her for the call and hung up, amazed and touched that he had actually remembered and taken the time in his incredibly busy schedule to ask the secretary to let me know.

I wondered at the time why this call had meant so much to me. After all, I had never expected him to actually find me shoes, and I had already gone ahead and decided on a pair of shoes for Billie. Looking back, I think that this moment shone out so brightly because it put the spotlight on an individual who was responsible even in the most difficult of situations. Here was an individual who followed up on a commitment, who understood, and who could be relied upon. Here was an individual that I actually could trust.

When the performance was over, the director referred to me as "the glue that held the project together." As it turned out, there was a film director in the audience opening night who also loved Billie and wanted a similar character for a film he was producing. Novice actor though I was, I would soon be taking the supporting lead role in a new, independent film.

seven
Playing Lucy

Vertigo and a Dilemma

My first professional job offer as an actor—to play Lucy Dickson, a housekeeper, in the film *Vertigo*—created a personal and ethical dilemma for me. I had always said that I would only do work that generated positive feelings in the world, feelings of higher vibrations, reflecting the vision of a shifted worldview. But now, here I was about to act in, of all things, a horror film.

I accepted the role because of the work that the director of *Balm in Gilead* did to open this door for me. It was largely because of his kind and praising words of me that the film producer offered such a key role to a beginner. Because of the director's confidence and faith in me, and his work in opening the door for me, I felt I must do the role based on my love and respect for this most inspiring teacher.

Somehow, I would have to work my way through the dilemma. My job as an actress in the horror movie was to immerse my character (and being!) in fear. As in the preparation work for Billie, I was challenged to voluntarily stimulate feelings of intense fear and panic. I had read enough work on the molecules of emotion to know precisely what immersing myself in this emotion meant for my body, and the bodies and spirits of my audience who would also feel my fear if I did my job right. Did I really want to put more fear into the world? It seemed totally opposed to my original intentions for exploring the arts. Yet, I did it for my friend.

Fortunately, it turned out to be incredibly wonderful for me to work with this cast and crew. For example, one day while shooting, my director friend had told me offhandedly to look at the faces of the young people involved in making the horror film. So, one day when we all went out to dinner together, I did look closely at their faces. Each and every one of them radiated light. They were so beautiful. They were all in their 20s and 30s, and all doing the project for the same reason as I was: out of love and loyalty and dedication to the two men whose vision this movie was. Like me, none of them would see any money for their efforts unless the movie sold. My director friend had told me that the movie was being done "for the right reasons" and I now understood what he meant. It was being done for love of fellow artists and love of the craft and art of making movies.

I found myself renewed, rejuvenated, and re-inspired by the commitment and dedication of this crew of young people. In many ways it was a healing counterpoint to the lack of professionalism that I had just been through. It gave me confidence in the work ethic of the youth of today.

Purple Mist

The most profound unexpected result of doing the horror movie happened during the death scene that my character was required to do. In this scene, my character, Lucy (a gossipy woman who cleans as a housekeeper for a living) is found dead in an attic. For the shoot I was required to lie on my back in a small attic crawlspace. The officer and his partner look in, find me dead, and confirm it.

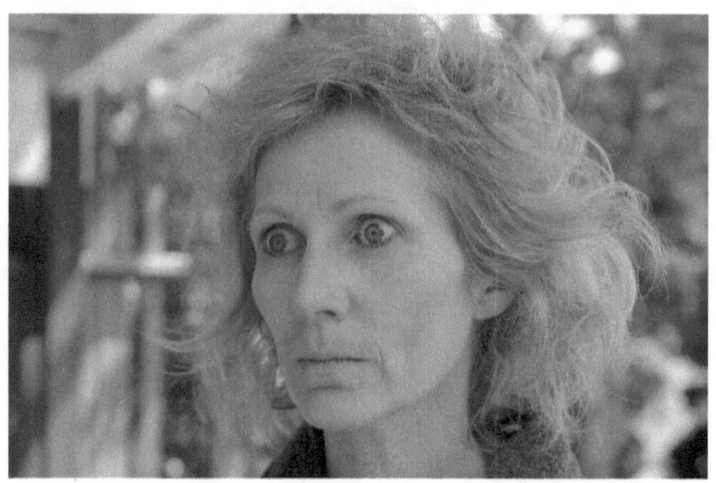

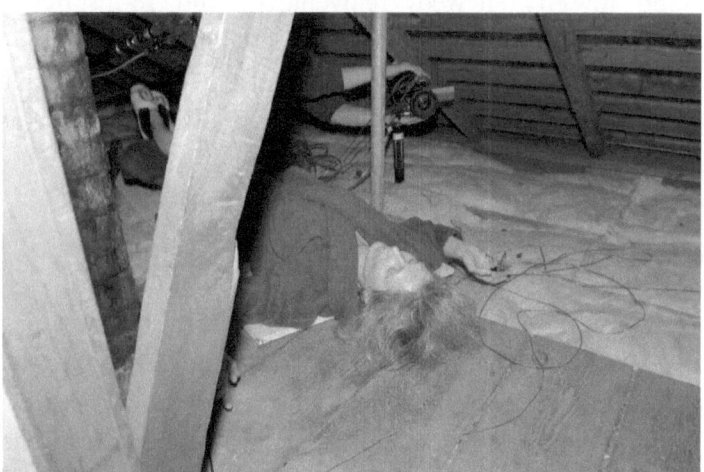

**Lucy Dickson, played by Duanita Gaye, in *Vertigo*,
directed by David Tamagi;** *photographs by John Molnar*

During the shoot that day, a still-life photographer was there, capturing stills of cast and crew. When he took a couple of pictures of me as Lucy, "dead," the director got inspired and asked him to pretend that he was a police forensic photographer so that we could get some footage of that. From behind my closed lids I could see the lights flashing rapidly as the scene was shot, and I began my inner monologue. I had decided to work with all of the research I had done on near-death experiences (NDEs) and what people report seeing and experiencing during periods of time when the spirit "leaves" the body and the body is officially dead. I worked with the flashes of light from the photography to begin myself imagining seeing "the light" and going through a long, long tunnel until it was getting brighter and brighter. I allowed myself to fully sink into this experience and found myself very detached from the scene being acted out around me.

After the shoot was over, the photographer came up to me and asked, "Want to see something freaky?" I said, "Sure." Then he showed me one of the digital images that he had taken of me as Lucy, "dead" on the floor. In it there was a purple-colored haze or mist or cloud rising up from my body. It originated in the area of my heart, floated up over my face, and began to dissipate just above my head. The image below is just one of many shot during that scene.

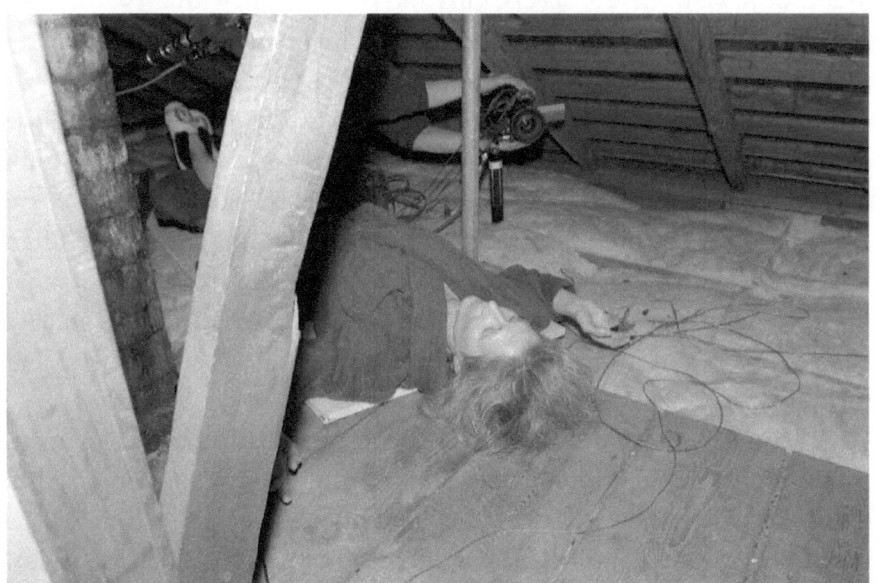

Purple mist over the death scene of Lucy in *Vertigo*;
photograph by John Molnar

For me, the image was a sign—a confirmation that I had really reached a profound level in being able to act a death scene, and since this was my first death scene ever, this confirmation was important to me. I later joked with my acting teachers that I knew that I did very well, and that I was going to specialize in being a dead actor.

Duanita G. Eleniak, PhD

A New Way of Seeing

Like the purple mist in Lucy's death scene, light spheres and similar images appearing in photographs have been documented elsewhere. The theory is that new technologies (for example, digital cameras) pick up such "apparitions" because, unlike us, the camera is dispassionate and records the world without the filters of belief systems and preconditioned ideas. Cameras are therefore much more objective in their capturing of "reality."

In my own private practice as an art therapist, I sometimes take pictures of children and/or their artwork for their personal journals that we keep as part of the case record. Over time, I have seen many instances of light (of various colors and shapes) being recorded on these images. I have come over time to view these as special gifts and I often work with these recorded instances of light for the purposes of healing. For example, I remember such a chance happening being recorded in a picture I took of a hurt, abused, and neglected nine year-old girl who was coming to me because she was very depressed. When I saw the light in the image radiating from her right side, I was delighted and she was amazed. She chose to believe that this was a picture of her Guardian Angel and her spirits were lifted immediately. She took the picture home as a concrete piece of evidence that she need never feel alone again, that she was being watched over, guided, and protected, and that she always had someone that she could talk to and turn to for help.

The unexpected result of my experiencing a death scene as an actor, with a ghostlike apparition emanating from my body captured on film, sparked a whole new series of thoughts about the use of film in the intentional creation of stories that might facilitate shifts in consciousness. Why not, for example, use cameras to help us avoid the pitfall of paradigm blindness? In the movie *What the Bleep Do We Know!?* (2004), the story is told of how indigenous peoples at first did not see Columbus's ships in the harbor. It was the wise people of the tribe that saw them first, based on physical indicators and their ponderous efforts. Because of the people's trust in these wise members of their worlds, they too were eventually able to see the ships. The people did not initially see the ships because they did not expect to see them. As a result, the ships remained outside of their field of observation.

I wonder what "ships" are currently out there that a majority of us are failing to see, but which would change the world as we know it forever if our eyes were to be opened to these realities. I wonder about the role that technology, specifically digital film, can play in making these realities visible to us in an obvious, concrete, undeniable way. I wonder what images cameras are already capturing that might assist the shift in worldview—if we only open our eyes to such images. How might we use cameras to enhance the power of film and television as transformational tools?

Without doubt, the Lucy experience gave me a new appreciation of technologies in the arts. I think that, independent of us, they have capacities to capture subtleties that we can only begin to understand and that they are valuable aids, particularly in pioneering explorations of effective means to transform consciousness. Technologies allow for an "objective" observer, limited only by our ability to see and appreciate what they are able to capture as reality.

Making *Vertigo* turned out to be a positive experience, one that I hoped to repeat as I moved further into the filmmaking phase of my coursework. But what I encountered instead were stumbling blocks at every turn.

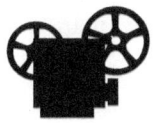

eight
Through the Looking Glass of Film

Third Test: Four 24-Hour Film Shorts

In the third semester of the program, the final project was to write and act in two short films. The films were to be developed in 24 hours spread over 6 weeks (of four-hour classes). They were to be no more than 10 minutes in length. Additionally, we were asked to crew two of our classmates' film shorts.

The final films were edited and placed on a graduation CD. One film would be chosen as the winner of the 24-hour short film competition. My involvement in this third test included writing and acting in two film shorts—I was "Diana" in *Gypsy Eyes* and "Ivy Pepper" in *Cleaning House*. I also acted and crewed in my classmates' two films, playing the roles of "Dr. LoveJoy" in *Infected* and "Principal" in *525,000 Minutes*.

Together, these four films were a looking glass, reflecting back the joys and disappointments of the creative process, the tensions of working in a group, and my own personal struggles and triumphs.

Film #1—Gypsy Eyes

After *Balm in Gilead*, a one-week rest during semester break did much to replenish my reserves and restore my positive attitude. In fact, the initial cast meeting for the first short film had my heart singing and my hopes raised high. The cast members in attendance were easily able to assign the responsibilities (executive producer, writer, location person, wardrobe and props, transportation, and catering) for the successful creation of a film. We were also able to come up with a production company name, "Choolikeit Productions." We all agreed on a storyline and were able to roughly sketch out characters that would fit each actor in the group. We accomplished an incredible amount of work in a short period of time and, most important of all to me was the fact that we did it in a spirit of harmony and cooperation. We were laughing and having fun as we brainstormed ideas and possibilities.

The next meeting was set to occur at the location we thought we could film at, my studio. I had been named executive producer and head writer. I committed to writing a first draft of the script based on the ideas we had imagined during the first meeting—within the week—in order to come with a base on which to improvise scenes and dialogue at the following meeting. Time was of the essence, since the rough draft needed to be complete for class review in the third week.

As promised, I took the storyline and character ideas that the group had brainstormed and wrote the first draft of the script. Once again, I found myself pleased and delighted with the process. I had written one screenplay previous to this and I saw how much better a screenplay writer I had become as a direct result of my training as an actor. The whole world of actor training that I was immersed in, though based in writing and scripts, had often seemed distant from the art of writing. Now I rejoiced both in my return to writing and the obvious strides that acting had created in my work.

I was very proud of the first draft as I handed it to all group members for their review and study, in preparation for improv and scene revision at the next group meeting. The story unfolded through the eyes of a gypsy psychic who could read into people's past and future. I loved the idea of incorporating many levels of reality and playing with the dominant worldview's linear concept of time. I went to the second group meeting with much joy in my heart. The story was coming together on schedule and harmoniously. The purpose of the second meeting was to improvise dialogue as written in the script in order to tighten the scenes and ultimately the story. It was also a time for us to check out the location, brainstorm about props, and decide where to best shoot each scene.

The group members that had missed the initial planning meeting of the film were at the meeting. These two classmates ended up teaching me very significant lessons. When asked for their input into the script, one of them, whom we'll call "Rose," just shrugged and said, "It's OK." The other classmate—we'll call her "Socks"—began to critique the believability of the story. The group clarified that this was a first draft and we could change anything and everything in it, including the story itself. Yet, given this invitation for change, neither of these classmates wanted to contribute. I even offered to change characters for them if they wanted, because I could sense that one of them in particular felt her role in the movie was too minor. They reassured me that it was OK and that they were ready to improvise scenes. The improvisation of the scenes went well and the dialogue was refined. I wrote all of the changes into Rough Draft #2, which was to be presented the following week in class.

The teacher-peer class review resulted in one major observation: the story needed a clearer heroine and a tighter journey. The story should be told through someone's eyes and that someone must go through more of a transformation. As written, the story of a wise gypsy woman, and what she sees, did not allow for enough transformation of character. One comment completely threw me. Almost casually, the instructor told us we had done a great job and then reminded us to remember that at this point "nothing is sacred" in the script.

In retrospect I can see that the instructor most likely meant nothing, but his comment devastated me at the time. I had left the second meeting very frustrated. Though the work had gotten done, every alarm bell in my being was ringing. I felt that Rose and Socks were unhappy with the film and/or their roles in it. This situation really bothered me but I was unable to address it, because if I brought anything up, they both would tell me everything was okay.

Several days before the rough-draft presentation of the script to the class, the co-executive producer of the film came into the classroom after a break, just livid with anger. She had ridden down in the elevator with Rose, and Rose had told her that she hated the film, hated her character, and really did not want to do it. The co-executive producer was shocked and then angry that none of these strong feelings had been expressed openly the week before in our meeting when there had been plenty of opportunity.

My intuitive feelings were confirmed. All was not harmonious under the surface. Before the script presentation to the class, I wondered long and hard about what to do in this situation. Should I bring this dynamic up to the surface in the group or just let it boil underneath the whole project? If "nothing was sacred," what about all the hard work that had been done already? And what about the deadlines coming up quickly for rehearsal times and then shooting?

After our feedback on the script, we moved as a group to the other room to discuss where to go next. I felt awful sitting in the group. It felt like such a lie to be sitting there with two group members unhappy to the point of "hating" a project, yet smiling and nodding and saying everything was okay. The struggle that I had been feeling about whether to bring this up seemed to reach a conclusion even without my conscious consent when I heard the words "nothing is sacred." I began with those words and said that anything and everything could still be thrown out in the script. I said that I knew both Rose and Socks were very unhappy with the project and now was the time to change it.

Total chaos broke out. Rose denied that she felt strong dislike for the project. Socks just seemed shocked and then began coming up with new ideas for a film, which led the group in several dead-end directions. The other group members that had been happy about the process were dismayed that I brought up the issue. Our teacher, who had dropped by to check on the group, later said that he was shocked that we were even considering throwing all our work out.

I wondered why I did this, even as I did it. I could have predicted the denial on Rose's part and the inability of Socks to have come up with anything better by way of a script. The cracking open of the discontent lying under the surface just led to everyone feeling badly—the four of us who had put work into the script and who loved it, and the two that were being extremely negative. At the end of that meeting we decided that our script would be shelved and that Socks and Rose could come up with some ideas that they would be happy with, turn them into me, and I would write something up by the following week when we needed to "pitch" the film idea to the director.

Everyone left the meeting feeling terrible. I had taken the words "nothing is sacred at this point" and had single-handedly, through my power as a leader, destroyed all the strides and goodness that had been accomplished to that point. In reflection, I think that something broke in me when the instructor said "nothing is sacred". I was hurt by that comment and did not think it accurate. Inwardly, I was angry that he could say this about the work that we had so lovingly done—and which we had enjoyed doing. Yet I can see now that I gave in, despite my feelings to the contrary, because of an old pattern of mine, which is to think that the teacher is always right. He is more experienced, so if he says that anything and everything can still go at this point, then he must be right.

The bad feelings that I had that night led me to reconsider the decision we had made to throw the whole thing wide open again. We were working with a time constraint; we had a pretty decent script already, which simply needed to be tweaked; a majority of the team were really happy with the script; the two members who were unhappy had failed to give any useful input to the process; and, most importantly, the work ethic that Rose and Socks had so far displayed implied that giving them full responsibility to come up with something else this late in the game was simply foolhardy.

I realized that the teacher was either wrong or that I had misinterpreted what he said and took it more literally than he intended. I decided to follow my gut—declare the main ideas of the script sacred and adhere to the main intentions we had set out. I decided that I would do one more rewrite, incorporating the feedback given during the review of the first draft. The co-executive producer and I met with the teacher, who gave us full permission to take the script forward regardless of the two group members' unhappiness. He then instructed me to "step up to the plate" as the co-executive producer, take my power, and make decisions. He told us that if we still got resistance from the team members, we had the authority to do what we needed to do and that he would support us in our decision. We announced to the team that the original ideas were back on the table, and I began rewriting.

This was challenging because, basically, the whole point of view (POV) of the storyline had to be reformulated. A clear heroine/hero needed to be identified. I went to my keyboard having no idea how I was going to do this and still have Esmeralda, the gypsy, in mind as the heroine. In Draft #1 it was her story, the story of a wise woman who can see into the past and the future, and who helps other women prevent abusive relationships. What happened when I went to the keyboard, however, changed everything. As

I played with different ideas about how to sharpen the drama and intensity of the heroine's journey, I suddenly got the idea that the whole of Draft #1 was actually a dream—the dream of the man in the script, Jean-Pierre.

I went with the idea and was struck with how easy this change of perspective made the revisions. With the addition of a new introductory scene and concluding scene, the tasks of sharpening the point of view and increasing the transformative journey of the hero was accomplished. It also added another level of depth to the script, one that is a passion of mine. Suddenly the movie was a statement on the value, importance, and transformational ability of our dreams.

I was very excited about the script changes and felt really confident because of how easily they had come together after I had the inspiration. I gave the team members and our instructor the revised script. This we were to pitch to the director in four days' time.

What I went through in the rewrite really speaks to the magic of the creative process. Based on an inspiration that came from nowhere, revisions flowed easily. Due to a deadline, the changes were set. It happened so quickly and when we explore the "it," we see that the story changed drastically in the rewrite almost as if it had a life of its own. The "minor revisions" transformed the whole story. It was Jean-Pierre's story now rather than Esmeralda's. It was a story of a lying, cheating fiancé having a powerful dream that helps him to recognize the folly of his ways and commit himself in integrity to the good woman to whom he is engaged. It amazes me how POV, as writers refer to it, changes everything about a story. The shift in POV created a shift in the roles of the characters and therefore in the responsibilities of the actors.

It was now time to schedule rehearsals. Based on our time after the pitch to the director (which, if passed, would be the final approval of the script), and before the filming, we had exactly two weeks for rehearsals. We held a meeting at which five out of the six members of the team were present. "Jean-Pierre" had been missing classes and was unavailable for the scheduling meeting. Based on the five team members' schedule, a rehearsal schedule was set.

One of the main issues that had been causing problems on this team was attendance: people simply not being present when decisions were being made. When the rehearsal schedule was set, it was made clear that everyone needed to be there. Rose and Socks stated all of their difficulties with rehearsing on the two Sundays. The problem was that the two Sundays were turning out to be the only time in everyone's schedules that rehearsals and set decoration could happen before filming. Someone asked about Jean-Pierre and what would happen if he could not make these rehearsal times. Based on the meeting with the teacher, and the strategy that had been set out to deal with the absenteeism issue, the other executive producer and myself set a very clear guideline. The rehearsal times would remain, since they were the only ones available. If the cast could not attend, other actors from outside the group would be called in to do the part and the actor that could not attend would be written a more minor role that required no, or less, rehearsal. Everyone present at the meeting agreed to this as fair and the group decided that I would present this decision and the rehearsal schedule to Jean-Pierre the next day.

When I presented the rehearsal schedule to Jean-Pierre, he immediately said that he could not attend rehearsals on the Sundays because he was working. I told him that in that case, what we were going to do was get someone else to play Jean-Pierre and we would write him a more minor role. He got very angry at this and said that he wanted to do the role but could not rehearse on those days. I informed him that these were the only times when a majority of the group could come, and we had made the decision that if cast members couldn't make it, we were rewriting their roles, because rehearsing was important. To this, he replied that the role was "easy" for him and he did not need to rehearse. This comment really made me angry. I told him that this role was not "easy"—that indeed, with the rewrites, it was the lead character. He was in every scene. Without him at rehearsals, no one could rehearse the scenes. There were many lines to learn and an important character to develop.

He got very angry with me and simply would not accept the decision that the group had made. When he called me a "bitch," I told him I would take up the matter with the instructor.

As I went to the instructor's office, the actor followed me and entered with me. I explained to the instructor the decision that the group had come to and the times that were available to rehearse. The actor explained that he could not make those times. What happened then left me floored. Instead of the instructor supporting us in our decision to enforce attendance, he began negotiating with the actor. "So you have to work on Sundays. And you have child support to pay, so the money is important. Well, maybe you could arrange to go to one of the rehearsals instead of two. How about that as a compromise?" The actor agreed.

I was dumbfounded. I had been asked to "step up to the plate" and enforce decisions. I had been told that I would be supported in that authority yet, clearly, this was not the case. It did not really matter what we as executive producers decided; we really had no power to fire someone who was not pulling their weight. It was a pseudo-position with all of the responsibility, yet none of the power.

After the meeting, the other co-executive producer and I met to discuss what we would do with rehearsal times. The instructor came up to us and told us that he felt we were being too hard on the actor. I felt like I had been punched in the stomach.

I was infuriated with my instructor's line of thought, because everyone was making sacrifices of work and income to be able to film the movie. I was giving up a full day of work, as were others, and I was a single-parent mom having to support a daughter on my own. The difference was that the other actors were doing what professional actors need to do—give up their day jobs when rehearsals and filming come up.

Because of the "compromise," one Sunday rehearsal time was cancelled. There was no point in the other five of us meeting, because a majority of the scenes involved Jean-Pierre. One of the actors said she was willing to work with Jean-Pierre to ensure that he knew his lines and could enunciate his words. Even this never happened because scheduling rehearsal time remained a problem. As a result, the cast had only one full rehearsal time the day before shooting—and, even then, Rose informed the cast that she would not be there the whole time.

As "executive-producer," I knew that I had no real power to change this. Even though it would be great if we could have rehearsed the scenes, it was not going to happen. I made peace with this situation by telling myself that often in movies, actors rehearse alone and the first time they do a scene is in front of the cameras. And that was basically what happened with the filming of *Gypsy Eyes*.

I had written the film as a romantic comedy/drama; however, as it came to life during filming, it went over the top. The actor playing Jean-

Pierre, through his mannerisms, tone of voice, and body posturing, made a caricature out of the original conception of the character. The team members who had helped conceive the story intended Jean-Pierre to be a suave, debonair playboy. The actor took the character to extremes and made him ridiculous. I am not sure if this was done to compensate for not knowing the lines or the character, or if this was done intentionally. I do know that the director picked up on it and then directed the actor to exaggerate even further.

My experience as writer watching this happen was devastating. I said nothing. "Esmeralda" told "Jean-Pierre" that she felt he had ruined the whole story with his portrayal of the character. He was upset about the comment and came to me, wanting to know if I felt the same way. I could not speak.

My own experience acting across from him was horrendous. I was repulsed to my very core at the "slime-bucket" caricature that he oozed in his interpretation of Jean-Pierre. His hand movements, facial expression, and eye movements, when he would offer my character, Diana, his hand or his arm, made me cringe. I did not want him to touch me or be near me even in the scenes where I was supposed to be his naïve, dedicated, loyal fiancé. I was afraid that the camera would be picking up my true feelings, that I was not able to really connect with loving feelings while he was around in these scenes.

The whole filming process was extremely painful for me as a result of these reactions I was having to the main character. I watched as scene after scene developed into images that strayed from the original intention of the story. I felt helpless, hopeless, powerless, and choked.

I was grateful when the filming was over. I have only watched the end product once, at graduation, and I was sickened by it. It was so far from the original story, a spiritual romantic comedy about wise women and Casanovas done in a richness of color, look, and feel. Even after editing, I did not like the place where the film ended up, and I felt far less than proud to ever have been a part of creating it.

Film #2: Cleaning House

With only a couple of weeks to recuperate from the experience of making *Gypsy Eyes*, we were launched into our second 24-hour film short. For this project, the instructor decided to change the team selection process. He had hand selected our team for the first film; but now opted for luck of the draw, with names picked out of a hat. I felt relief when he told us how the teams were to be chosen. I knew that he had done his absolute best to make the first set of teams even, using his knowledge of our strengths. Because my team experience had been so intense, I now thought about whom I would want to be on a team with. My honest answer was none of my fellow students.

I disliked feeling this way and wondered if something was wrong with me. Were my expectations too high? Maybe my tolerance level was too low. But really, my ideal filmmaking team would be creative, intelligent artists who were professional and had a strong work ethic. They would come to work on time every time, contribute their ideas freely, stay until the work was finished, and have a high degree of integrity. They would be honest, truthful, caring, kind, loving, and supportive. I had the fortune to work with such a cast and crew in *Vertigo*, and I was grateful to know my ideal could be a reality.

After the names were drawn from the hat and the teams set, the students began complaining that the teams were too similar to the last ones we had worked on. Instead of standing firm on the results, the teacher allowed a second drawing from the hat. When this happened, I had a sudden flash of realization that the teacher had the same weakness that I struggled with—he wanted to please everyone. This had been one of my downfalls when I acted as executive producer in the first film. Our similarities in the issue helped me understand why the instructor had not supported our decision as executive producers to rewrite parts for the cast that were unable to attend rehearsals. He had fallen prey to his own need to keep everyone happy.

A second name draw turned out almost exactly the same as the first. To me this was a confirmation that the team groupings were accurate, because it was a synchronicity. The odds of the groupings remaining almost exactly the same were very low.

Again, the class grumbled, so the instructor took a vote on whether or not a third draw was necessary. I voted "no" but the majority wanted to pick again. For the third time the groupings remained quite similar to the teams we had been on in Film #1, so our instructor said that we could all choose to change teams just once. The dynamics around this conscious choice of team were interesting to watch. No one wanted to be with Socks. Some people chose to go with their friends. And one actor, who had previously declared a desire to work with me, but who had thought that it was highly unlikely this would happen, because we were both the more mature actors, took a long time choosing . . . even though another actor on the team was close to the actor. The actor finally chose to be on our team, and the teams were set. With the exception of this actor and one other, I was working with the same people as on the first project.

During our first meeting we assigned roles and responsibilities and discussed story and character possibilities. Immediately everyone wanted me to be executive-producer. Remembering my previous experience with this responsible, but powerless, position, I quickly refused. I argued that we needed to give everyone a chance at these roles and I had already been executive-producer, as had two others of the cast. That left the role of executive producer for "Jean-Pierre," Socks, or the other actress. Jean-Pierre and Socks did not want the responsibility, so the other actress took on the role with great trepidation; however, as it turned out, the role was a great boost to her self-confidence and self-esteem. Her incredible people skills were an asset.

I had decided that I no longer wanted to be responsible for everything in the production and was grateful to be excluded from this position. The role that I did accept was that of scriptwriter. I had enjoyed the magic involved with this process during our last film and was grateful to do it again. We then discussed ideas for the film and, as it turned out, two of the actors had already talked about wanting to do a film in the style of "film noir," in black and white. As ideas were exchanged, the concept of a black and white gangster movie in a gambling casino in about the 1920s was quickly born.

The two actors whose idea it was loved it; Jean-Pierre loved it because he was in reality a gambler; and the executive-producer loved it because she liked the type of wardrobe and hair she could wear. I liked it, too, because I could write myself in as the Casino singer, which meant playing a role connected to my idea of working with music and dance to transform consciousness. I also intended to develop a character and costume that I could use after I graduated, since I had begun thinking of creating some music sets. Not least of all for me, the role could be separate enough from the other characters that I did not have to get involved with rehearsal scheduling issues or lack of attendance at rehearsals. Socks, who was part of the team, was absent from school for the planning session and had no input into her character. The actors discussed various roles for her and wanted her in a minor role, because they were all concerned with attendance.

Writing the script was again a sheer joy for me. It was the first time that I had to study a period for a piece of writing. I researched costumes in the '20s, the "lingo" used, and the actual history of underground casinos in Chicago. Then I researched poker, because it is a game that I do not know. I had to very quickly go from knowing nothing of the game to being able to develop the best card game that could take the movie to its climax within 10 minutes and be very easy to shoot.

I also had to orchestrate and write in a gunfight, which was very challenging on many levels. The first level of challenge was whether I ethically wanted to write a scene where people are shot and killed. I questioned myself about whether or not I was promoting violence and felt bad that the movie would actually be resonating at a very low level of consciousness in terms of content. I decided to do it anyway and only hoped that the film's aesthetics would make up for the content.

I wrote my character, Ivy Pepper, into a minor role at the introduction and conclusion. I was very grateful to write in the first scene where I would be singing "Big Spender" in the Casino when the heroine "Sadie" walked in. This would give me a chance to showcase my singing abilities and give me footage that I could use as a demo when I finished school.

The script came together easily. Socks ended up cast in an important role as a server in the gambling house. In the story it is revealed that she is actually the secret girlfriend of Carlos, the gambler, who had been cheating in the gambling house for quite some time. The plot later reveals that she and Carlos had a plan to rob the gambling house that evening. Despite the actual importance of her role, Socks took an immediate dislike to it, because she felt it was too small.

The script passed the first reading with the entire class, except that the instructor wanted it shortened to ensure that is was held at 10 minutes. After discussing how this could be done in the easiest way possible, I informed the group that we would cut the current introduction scene and move directly to the backroom gambling scene. This would cut about two extra settings and reduce the time of shooting and overall running time of the script significantly. It would also be an easy cut to make without affecting the storyline. The only things eliminated would be an initial atmosphere setting for the casino and my main role in the film. My entire song performance was cut. Though there was some objection to this by the other actors, it was easy to see that this was the simplest solution. We compromised by deciding that I would still be filmed singing and that this would be rolled under the credits at the end.

I made the changes to the script and it was time to pitch the idea to the director. We came up with a great pitch line: *"How Do Three Dames Clean House?—BANG."* The executive director and I fielded questions, since I knew the script so well.

At this meeting, something happened of which I was unaware at the time. During the meeting, Socks put her head down on the desk and went to sleep. The other cast members noticed and attempted to rouse her—because her behavior was entirely unprofessional and inappropriate—but to no avail. This incident sealed the initial tone toward Socks that the others had begun during the first meeting. The tone was resentful and exclusionary. Socks became the black sheep of the group. She was the target of insults, usually uttered by most members of the group behind her back and by a few to her face. When wardrobe decisions were being made, there was no help for her.

It was difficult to help her. Her lack of attendance, forgetfulness of instructions, and critical attitude toward her role in the play all made it difficult to feel supportive of her. Even her body mannerisms—for example, shifting eyes that never really allowed you to look her in the eye—created barriers to connecting with her. Though this dynamic between Socks and the cast existed, I stayed largely out of it, because my speaking role in the movie was so small. I was glad to be totally uninvolved in rehearsal-time scheduling, making sure people came to rehearsals, and all of the other dynamics that had caused me so much grief during our first film. I completed the script, and the scene rehearsals were left to them.

I focused on finding the music and an image for my character, Ivy Pepper. Because I was intending on pursuing musical performance after graduation and actually had intentions of selling an act to the local casinos (because they have very nice theaters), I really poured myself into creating Ivy Pepper. I began with images of women from that era—their hair, makeup, and clothing. A Marilyn Munroe-ish/ Sophia Loren style became the guide.

I required a community of helpers to create Ivy Pepper. One of the hair/makeup students at the school, Yuko, was in charge of my hair and makeup. About one week before filming, Yuko did a practice run on my hair and makeup to time how long it would take. We had pictures of 1920s hairstyles from which she worked. After about two hours, the transformation into Ivy Pepper was complete and I was about to experience the power of beauty.

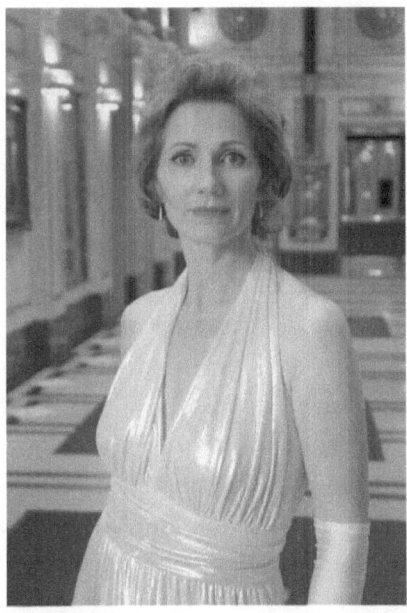

Ivy Pepper, played by Duanita Gaye, in *Cleaning House*, New Image College Of Fine Arts Student Film; *photograph by Trevan Wong*

When I walked out of the school as Ivy Pepper, with the makeup and the hair, people stared at me. It took me awhile to realize that it was because of the beauty Yuko had created. I had never experienced anything like it in my life. Both men and women were actually turning their heads on the street to get a look at me. Doors were opened for me. Crowds on the sidewalk began to part.

At one point I began to physically feel a different vibration in my body. I felt my center lower into my pelvis and I felt my legs and feet more as I placed them consciously on the sidewalk. This sensation and awareness amazed me, because usually when I walk, I just walk—unaware of the angle of my feet or the sway of my hips. I realized that I actually was swaying my hips, whereas usually my hips remained quite locked when I walked.

The part of me that was aware of all that was happening was very excited because I knew that I had found the character of Ivy Pepper in my very body. I was experiencing what it felt like to be Ivy Pepper, to live in her skin, in her body . . . and it was the most amazing sensation. I realized that I was really experiencing what the teachers had meant by the "center" and the magical transformation of character that can happen when that clicks in. In that stroll down two city blocks from the school to my car as Ivy Pepper, I realized the power of aesthetics and of beauty, and I experienced myself as a sexy woman for the first time in my life.

Part of the process that led up to my contacting the New Image School of Fine Arts was an insight into the fact that in order for me to be the most effective and powerful instrument for changing the current worldview, I needed to address what I had discovered to be a personal blind spot of mine: the way I presented myself physically—my clothes, hair, face, nails, wardrobe, and way of standing. Throughout my life I had operated from the belief system that it was what I knew and who I was that mattered, rather than how I looked. Though I ensured that I was always clean and well-groomed, I never paid any more conscious attention to my appearance. If I ever saw a woman using her appearance to get her further, I would judge the display as manipulation, and I simply wanted nothing to do with it.

In fact, looking back, I would need to say that, if anything, I downplayed my personal beauty. I hid behind big glasses, big sweaters, and plain clothes. I did this for many reasons. Sometimes I dressed down in order to "meet" the clients I was working with at the time, who lived in poverty—for example, when I worked in battered women's shelters, with downtown eastside Natives or with street kids. Sometimes I dressed down to attract no sexual attention to myself, particularly if I was in a relationship with someone. This denial of my sexual attractiveness went even deeper with a belief system that while I could be pretty, I could never be a knock-out stunning beauty because then I would be vain and people would think I'm a bitch. I can look back now and see the very real fear I had of actually expressing my sexuality in an aesthetic, physical way with my body.

I had been told that I would not be fully effective or working at my fullest potential unless I paid more conscious attention to this area. At first I resisted but finally I broke down and did a little research, and I found out that, indeed, it is often what you look like rather than what you know that gets you the attention of people. At first, the research enraged me, but as I began to educate myself in the area of aesthetics, I realized that actually working consciously with hair, makeup, nails, and wardrobe could be in the service of a higher value—that of beauty. I realized that working with line, shape, and color on my body was creating archetypes that people responded to powerfully.

Even though all of these insights had come to me, and I had accepted the fact that this was a worthwhile area that I needed to develop, I was having trouble. On a personal level, I struggled to actually *feel* and believe that I was sexy and beautiful. I would hear people say it, and I even began affirming it, but I never really *felt* it—until that walk as Ivy Pepper.

Finding the character of Ivy Pepper inside me and experiencing her gave me an opportunity to really feel sexy in every cell of my being. I understood how deeply powerful I was in my sexiness and beauty. For the first time in my life I really believed I was sexy and I was comfortable with that knowledge. This was an incredible breakthrough for me.

The hair and makeup were complemented by Janet Dundas at the Black Fly, who designed a gown for Ivy Pepper. It was made of silver shimmering material, because I had been told that this color would work the best on film shooting in black and white. I had been told that I would be filmed singing under high contrast lights, solo, with a microphone. The silver dress with silver strappy shoes and long white gloves would create a '20s glamour effect.

Because I knew that I might be able to use the Ivy Pepper image as promotion for my singing work after I graduated, I asked permission for the photographer who did my headshots to come and take some pictures of me in full costume on the day we were filming. The instructor gladly agreed and even suggested offhandedly that we could make up movie posters. I loved the idea and, on the day of filming, the still photographer came, did promotional shots of me, took movie shots of us three "dames," and then even shot pictures of the entire cast and the filming.

As it turns out, the photographs were a great hit and the school now uses them as promotional material. I was extremely grateful that I did hire the photographer to come in, particularly when I walked onto the set and saw the beauty that several of the other cast members had created. They had put much time, attention, and money into getting a great poker table, light, and a "smoke" machine to create a genuine feel of a backroom gambling place in the 1920s. I am grateful that their creation was captured on film.

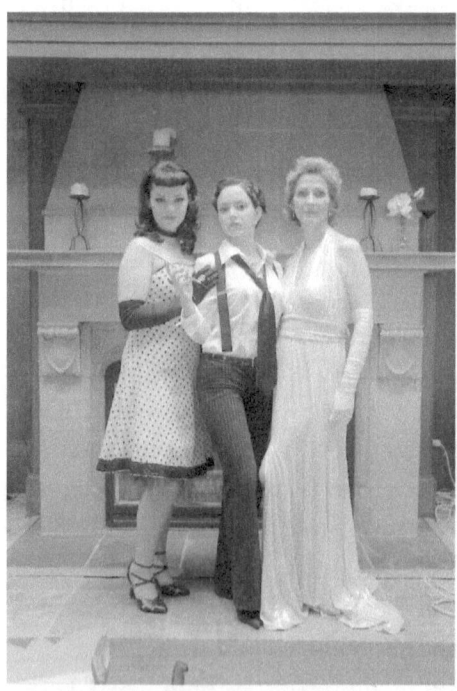

Ivy Pepper and friends, in *Cleaning House*, New Image College of Fine Arts Student Film; *photograph by Trevan Wong*

The actual day of filming was another incredible experience for me. One of the most powerful experiences I had that day as an actress was in working with atmosphere. Ivy Pepper had only one very short speaking scene. For the rest of the time I was in the background while the poker scene was being shot. This gave me plenty of time to relax and practice two methods we had been taught, "creating atmosphere" and "radiating." It was the most intriguing experience I have ever had on the power of silence and being active while, on the outside, it may seem that one is doing nothing.

What I was doing was running inner dialogues based on what was being said in the room—thinking exactly what Ivy Pepper would have been thinking. Sometimes in breaks, I would imagine a color or a feeling radiating out from me and filling the room with a particular atmosphere—tension, playfulness, sexual electricity.

At one point in the filming, one of the actors looked over at me and said, "You know, Ivy, for a gal who doesn't say anything, you sure do have a presence." I almost fell off my stool. It was confirmation and validation for me that what I was doing in my mind intentionally was being felt and experienced by others. I was so grateful for his comment because it encouraged me to continue (and sometimes after hours and hours and hours of filming in a smoky room, a bit of encouragement to keep going is most welcome—especially when the work is so internal). I asked him to say more about what he was experiencing. He said that even though he could not see me from his position on set, he was very aware of my presence behind him, that I felt like a white light filling the room. I was so grateful for his comments and for the opportunity to have such a long time to actively practice these skills.

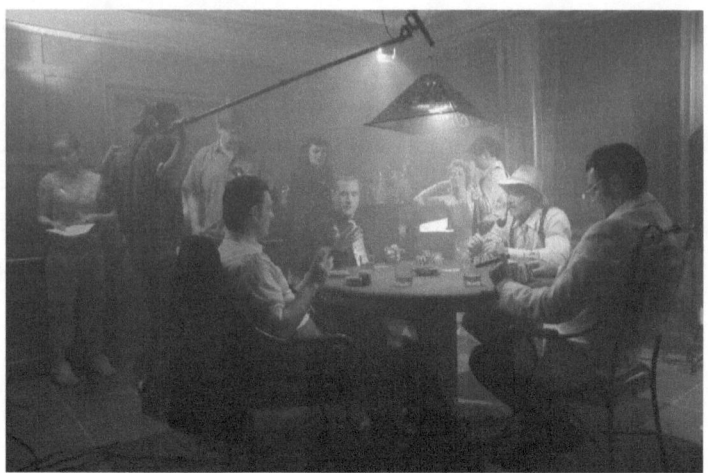

Radiating and creating atmosphere: Duanita Gaye as Ivy Pepper (background under the hanging light), in *Cleaning House*; photograph by Trevan Wong

The other invaluable experience that happened to me that day was as a writer. I had the opportunity to see how the creative process works in action on a film set and how the script actually becomes only a blueprint. Once actors and directors lift the words off the page, they have a life of their own, as does the story. This became particularly apparent during the filming of the shooting scene. I watched as action that I had painstakingly written and choreographed like a dance to match the characters and the story, just went flying out the window. Instead of following the words on the script like a recipe for the best gunfight ever, I watched as the creative process took over and it became an improv dance of *"How about we do this?" "No, how about this?"*

The same last-minute changes happened with Ivy Pepper's song. After all my rehearsal time, hiring a voice instructor and getting lessons, and having the music recorded by a pianist in town, there was a last-minute decision to cut the singing scene. I was both truly disappointed and truly relieved at the same time. It was the end of a long day of filming in a heavy smoke den atmosphere and my throat felt like the inside of a stovepipe. Part of me just wanted to go home. The other part of me could have cried at the lost opportunity.

Films #3 and #4

The next two films were only supposed to involve me as a crew member, helping with food services, set decoration, and so on. As it turned out, for both films, I was asked to do a role. In *Infected* I played "Dr. Lovejoy" who delivered the results of a test to a group of passengers, telling them that they were not infected by a deadly virus and therefore they would live. In *525,000 Minutes* I was the owner of the school doing a speech at graduation. I thoroughly enjoyed preparing and delivering both roles.

These final two films gave me a real taste of what working on films is like, which I can sum up in one word—unpredictable. *Infected* shot for about 20 hours with very few breaks. It seemed a simple script; however, as one person put it, the director "shot the hell out of it!" *525,000 Minutes*, on the other hand, was shot in eight hours with very little direction or point of view shots taken. I realized how much impact the director's involvement has and how incredibly tiring the entire process from the other end of the camera, that is crewing, can be.

After the films were shot, the director edited them. The final versions were to be shown to all in attendance on graduation night. One film would be chosen that night as the winner of the 24-Hour Short Film Competition. I felt my anticipation growing. Graduation was going to be quite a ceremony, I thought—a rite of passage not soon to be forgotten.

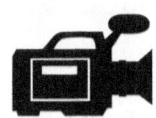

nine
Almost Full-out Glamour

Red-Carpet Grad Night

When the teachers asked us what we wanted for graduation night, I suggested striking a committee so that we students could do the planning. One student (who was quite responsible through the filming) volunteered to be the chairperson and organize committees to plan Grad. She asked me if I would chair the food committee and I agreed.

I spent considerable time on graduation planning and organizing the food. I got volunteers from class to bring sweets and salads. On our budget we bought chips, drinks, two catered trays, and a few other snacks. One volunteer brought tablecloths and candles. Everyone I spoke to was excited about graduation. I heard them talking about the decorating committee and having a red carpet. The planning committee decided that the event would be semiformal. Even Socks was excited. One day we happened to ride the elevator down from class together and walk a while. She seemed happy when she committed to bring her five-layer dip to contribute to the food table at Grad.

My personal preparation for graduation was elaborate. I realized that I most likely would have no formal ceremony upon completion of my doctoral program. Since this graduation really signified the completion of my field research for my PhD work, I decided to treat it as I would treat the completion of my doctorate. It would be the ceremony of the formal rite of passage. I had made it through three demanding tests and had learned so much beyond them, because I had gone through the program as part of my PhD research.

After many synchronistic happenings, I splurged and bought a red gown. I asked Yuko to do my hair and makeup. I decided to follow through on the visual that was part of some of the intentions with which I had been experimenting. At the beginning of the program, I had set intentions that I was an actress that combined qualities of such stars as Sophia Loren, Audrey Hepburn, Shirley MacLaine, and Julie Andrews. I committed myself to a dramatically classic image with my wardrobe combining classic pieces with a touch of flair in brooches, scarves, shoes, and accessories. Throughout the program I wrote affirmations in my Morning Pages that these qualities were already part of me.

As a result, on Grad night I decided to go almost full-out glamorous. I say "almost" because I held back on jewellery. Yuko did my hair up in a hive-style like Audrey Hepburn. She did my makeup in imitation of that style as well. I had decided to do my best to create what I had been visualizing and see what would happen.

The day before Grad I picked up a *Vanity Fair* magazine that a client had been thumbing through in my waiting room. I noticed that there was an article entitled "Tom Ford's New Hollywood: The 2006 Portfolio." Of most interest to me were the archetypal categorizations that he gave to people: "The Starling," "The Chameleon," "The It Girl," "The New Heart Throbs," "The Graduate," "The Beauty," "The Man's Man," "The Goddess," "The Reluctant Star," and so on. I thumbed through the article, holding in mind the intentions that I had been working with through the year as I invented or reinvented myself as an actress. I asked myself the question, which category would I be in? I decided that I would be featured under the category "The Touch of Class." The actress named in this role was Patricia Clarkson. It was "The Touch of Class" archetype that I intended to present at graduation.

A Class Act

The day of graduation came. I was excited. In my mind I was expecting Hollywood style, done Hollywood North style. I had heard some of the people talking about decorations and a pay bar, and I imagined an elegant, beautiful affair. I loaded my car with food, cards, and gifts for my peers, and my Grad outfit to change into after setting up the food.

When I got to the school, I immediately bumped into the teachers working hard on things like getting ice and getting the equipment prepared to play the movies. When I went into the school, however, I could see that very little had been done and no students were there helping. I was told that no one showed up, including the chair of the committee. The teachers had done what little decorating there was as a last-ditch attempt to salvage the evening.

This information and situation really disturbed me. I knew that the students had initially had great big ideas and really desired a beautiful event. What had happened? How come no students had really stepped forward to do the work necessary to create the beauty and container of the evening—the setting?

I set up the food and was very grateful to see that all of the students who had committed to bringing something had actually followed through. The only exception to this was Socks, who actually never showed up for the graduation at all.

My hair and makeup were done and I put on my dress. I took a deep breath and set forth into the graduation party. Despite all my work and intentions and affirmations the entire year, I still had a bit of a difficult time holding that level of glamour and class. In my life, I have simply never had people look and/or stare at me or make comments about my appearance. It was still somewhat difficult for me to come out, shining my best light as brightly as I possibly could, allowing myself to be seen in my full radiance of beauty.

That night I got a sense of what it is like to be an individual carrying a collective projection, like we ask our "stars" and "leaders" in society to do. The most wonderful, confirming synchronicity happened when I walked up to collect my diploma. One of the most respected teachers and Canadian actor/director/producers yelled from the audience, "A Class Act." At that moment I had a physical feeling of something moving down into my belly, like "thunk!" It was a physical feeling of realization that came along with a very deep sense that "I had done it." I was being recognized as "A Class Act." My inner intention to portray the archetype of "The Touch of Class" and my outer reality reflected each other. I had been given the gift of confirmation that it was so.

My image of graduation night and the reality of it, however, were very far from a match. The room chosen to see the movies in was hot, stuffy, and overcrowded. Many of the guests that came never got to see the movies. There had been an intention to have two viewings of the films; however, technical difficulties caused a long delay before the first viewing and after the viewing people were hot and tired. Though the teachers had even provided a D.J. for the evening, everyone left early and very few people actually danced.

Watching the films was very painful for me. It was difficult to watch myself in character. I was disappointed to see my name misspelled on the credits in all of the films. I had been particularly careful in writing my name down for the editor to assist him when doing the credits—to no avail.

I was also quite shocked to see the stories in their final version with special effects and music added. I was shocked to see how different they were from the original stories I thought I had been writing. I was further shocked to realize that what my teachers had told me was indeed accurate: films are made in the editor's studio. I recognized that if I were to use film as a medium for the transformation of consciousness, it would be necessary to have input into *all* the stages—writing, acting/directing, editing, and producing—to ensure that the information was delivered in alignment with highest intention.

The other shock I had was a realization that the two films on which I had been head writer had the exact same theme, women overcoming abusive/lying/cheating men by using masculine methods of power—that is, killing and dominance to the point of slavery. That night, I was dismayed at what I had taken part in creating.

And the shocks were to continue.

Student of the Year

The movie *525,000 Minutes* was really based on an actual award that was given out at the college at graduation. The award was called "Student of the Year." There had actually been quite a buzz going on with the students for some months prior to Grad, regarding who would receive this award. I had not paid much attention, because I have received my fill of awards and trophies in my life and I have lived long enough to have seen them collect dust, be broken, and somehow lose significance over the years, while the inner growth and accomplishment was what remained.

It was my daughter's question that prompted me to awareness of this award. She asked me, "Mommy, who do you think will win 'Student of the Year'?" So I went through each and every one of the students in terms of 1) professionalism and regular/consistent attendance; 2) reliability (doing their homework and coming prepared to school each day for their scenes); 3) commitment to learning; 4) ability to work with peers; and 5) attitude toward their profession and peers. While each student brought strengths in different areas, I had to honestly say that I would choose myself as student of the year—no contest. I could see that I was truly (as one of my teachers had acknowledged) "a role model as a student for everyone else in the class." I was a role model simply on the basis of what I was doing in the classroom. If you added in the fact that I was doing this while being a great single mom, handling a full-time career, and doing a PhD simultaneously, it pushed me into a "class of my own" or into the genre of "alien."

All of the students then began telling me spontaneously that they thought I would be student of the year. On Grad night one fellow student leaned over to me right before "Student of the Year" was announced and said, "Get ready; here is your award." The name was announced and everyone's jaw dropped. The name of the student sitting beside me was announced as "Student of the Year."

The rationalization behind this decision was that they awarded it to the student who had gone through the biggest "journey" over the course of the year. Well, indeed, my phenomenal journey was largely an inner quantum leap. No one had asked me about my inner journey. And on the outside I had simply been a consistently excellent student, though I would argue that even on the outside, my work had improved by leaps and bounds.

The actor that they chose as "Student of the Year" came up to me on several occasions and told me in all honesty that he felt I should have gotten the award. He knew his inner and his outer journey. In the outer journey, he began as a student who came fairly regularly and was excited and enthusiastic and, like all of us, had lots of creative blocks, particularly emotional, to overcome. During the last two months of the year he was a student who hardly came to class, came late, and often came very unprepared—even in audition sessions where outside people were judging his work.

His absence was so obvious that several students who came regularly, consistently, and at various levels of preparedness, began to comment on it. Their comments held grains of truth. They commented on how this actor was being excused from class to assist with the other class's filmmaking, something that they too would have liked to do but were never granted the opportunity. They felt it unfair. On one occasion during a film shoot, the instructor and director invited the actor who had been chosen "Student of the Year" out with them on break. Another student began to quip, "Hey, can I come with you, too? Why is it only him you ask?" I could understand that they asked him because they had been working on so many films together and they had created a bond. Yet I did note that an actress who had also been crewing for other classes rather than attending classroom studies was not invited.

What the students were implying was that there was favoritism going on. I could not help but notice that the theme of the movie *525,000 Minutes* had come very close to reality—that is, where a student who was no longer even in the school was chosen "Student of the Year." The movie was made as a "mockumentary" of our experiences at the school.

I am sure that the teachers looked at the "Student of the Year" actor's willingness to take major roles in the final films and take risks in these roles. While this is true, I think that, at the end of the day, instead of singling one student out, it would be wiser to ac-knowledge the unique contributions of each and every artist that graduated from the program.

The element of competition that was in the "Student of the Year" award carried over into the 24-Hour Short Film competition, for now one film was going to be chosen as the winner. Everyone who had seen the films was allowed to vote for which film they thought was the winner. The teachers would then declare one winner.

After seeing the movies and experiencing the dynamics of the spirit of competition with "Student of the Year" award, I decided to avoid voting for one film that I wanted to win. I could truly see that each film had something unique that it contributed. I could see that each was in such different categories and that judging them against each other did not even make sense. I could see that some of the restrictions within which we had worked—for example, keeping the short to a 10-minute final product—had been allowed to slide for some of the films. The unevenness between the films with regard to things like final air time and editing/filming hours devoted to its creation made me realize that there were very different starting lines for these films.

That graduation night, no decision was made because there were actually quite heated discussions among the teachers regarding which film should win. No agreement was reached. Weeks later, I learned through a chance meeting with the "Student of the Year" that the film of which he was executive director, *Infected*, had won Best Picture. The rationalization given was that the characters had the most "journey" in the film.

I know that the instructors struggled with their decision for "Best Film Short" and "Student of the Year." I know that they did their very best to choose wisely and carefully, working with all of their wisdom, experience, and intelligence. I am just left, however, truly, truly saddened to see the effects of working in the artist's community under an old paradigm of competition that fosters separation, alienation, scarcity, and discouragement.

Socks

Several weeks after graduation, I ran into a group of students who had continued in the advanced program. I listened as they spoke of Socks, how she never came to Grad and how she still did not even pick up her diploma. The next day, one of my old teachers called to tell me some dreadful news.

Socks had committed suicide.

How could this have happened? How could we all have missed the desperation of her soul? I was consumed by the fact that I'd had no idea. I was trained; I had watched her. I spent quite a bit of alone time with her. I did not know.

I had been as hard on her as I had been on Rose, the student who never showed up for rehearsals. Rose had openly said to me that she regarded me like the Mom she never had. At one point I had an intuitive flash of a reason that she was not at rehearsals. Because it was an intuition, and because it was of such a personal nature, I said nothing. During one of the final classes, time and space cleared. Because I was helping her prepare a particular role for an audition, she confided in me about her reason for absence. It was just as I had intuited. At least I had a knowing of why she was unavailable for rehearsals.

With Socks I had experienced no intuitive flashes. This tragedy has left a mark on me. I will always remember that sometimes I am working with far less than full information about a person's situation and that, despite people's behaviors, I must always continue to look for the light in everyone I see.

I was honored to have been part of the class—and relieved to escape the intensity of working together.

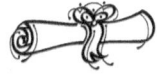

ten

Transformations and Reflections

Taking Stock

With Grad behind me, I felt that, in many ways, I was a different person from the woman who had first enrolled in acting classes. But, I wondered, to what extent had I actually undergone a shift in consciousness? Had I accomplished anything to assist a transition to a spiritual worldview? As it had more than once before, the answer came to me: "Look around you and see if anything has changed."

When I took stock of my life after my immersion in the per-forming arts, I could see that in several quite obvious ways a lot had changed. And the changes took in both the professional and personal dimensions of my life.

The New Studio

At the beginning of my immersion process, it unexpectedly happened that I needed to move my studio. I had worked in the same location for 10 years and loved my place. Suddenly, however, I was confronted with two new neighbors. One was a bartending school that set up the wall where they put their glasses away on the backside of one of my studio walls. The other was a dance school whose ventilation system happened to connect to mine and through which poured their music. Between the clinking of glasses and the loud music I knew that, though I had never thought I would leave, it was time for me to find a new studio. I eventually found my new space, which was double the size and two-thirds the cost of the original space. I moved in and began my practice there.

Several months later, my business license came up for renewal. I went to pay it as I always had, only to find that they refused to license me as a therapist in the new location. As it turns out, my move had taken me from the "city" to the "district," and the zoning restrictions allowed only light industry in that area, rather than professional practices. I was mortified. I had found out about the space through the professional that had rented it just prior to me. No one, including the landlord, could believe what was happening, because the zoning restrictions had never been enforced before. But now, for whatever reason, the district officials had decided to begin to enforce the zoning restrictions. I continued to do my daily work with intentions, affirming my creative work on my projects and myself, and affirming an imagination of the new space, as if it were easily licensed for me.

And then I found it. Deep in the section on exceptions in the bylaws was one clause that verified that a business license could be granted to a small artist studio in that area. In other words, I could no longer obtain a business license with my role as clinical social worker being paramount. Now the community would recognize and accept me only if I presented myself in the world as an artist, based on my credentials in art therapy.

This situation felt like a huge message from the Universe to me. For months I had been working on shifting my identity to that of an artist through images, affirmations, visualizations, and daily work as an actor. I had always had trouble seeing myself as, and calling myself, an artist. I always had identified with the "therapist" side of "art therapist" rather than the "artist" side. Yet I had known that I must be able to fully stand in the role of artist if I were to effectively work through the arts to assist shifts in consciousness. But how does one know if these intentions are working? How was I to know if the Universe was responding to the intentions and images on which I had been focusing my attention? How was I to know if what I was doing was actually shifting me into being an artist?

I had been asking for messages from the Universe. This whole situation with the move and licensing seemed to me to be the reply—and the Universe's confirmation that I was worthy of the title "artist." It was as if the Universe literally moved me into a new space and created a circumstance where I was able to accept my new identity as artist and realize that the community would accept it as well. I had changed from therapist to artist, just as I had intended, imagined, and "felt" my way to. I had changed from therapist to artist just as I had imagined in my work in *Emerging*. My private practice had shifted focus and intention as well as location.

A Change in Career

The change in my private practice also shifted my career. As well as being a social worker and an art therapist, I was now also a trained actor. I had even had a supporting lead role in an independent film. My life now included auditions and agents, as well as attending to hair and nails and wardrobe. I had worked diligently in my Morning Pages, affirming and feeling "as if" I were "a brilliant and prolific writer"; as if I could embody my sexuality like Sophia Loren; sing and dance and act like Audrey Hepburn and Shirley MacLaine; and sing like Izzy (Israel Kamakawiwo'ole), a Hawaiian singer whose sound instantly opens my heart. And I did it. I am out in the world as an actress with singing and dancing as my first loves.

As the succession of photographs taken of me before, during, and after completing the immersion project show, my physical appearance underwent marked change (see Chapter 2). Working with the concepts of intention and attention, I had been affirming the conscious creation of a "dramatically classic" look. This was something very new for me, because before the immersion project I had been unaware of the impact of my looks on people. It was simply an area where I paid little or no attention. During the immersion, I became aware of the impact of beauty and the alignment of beauty with Source Energy. I consciously began to align with this value. My wardrobe changed and I became more aware of what I was putting into it and why. Previously I had only looked for comfort as a factor in wardrobe selection. Now I am a conscious shopper aware of color, line, shape, and design—and the type of feelings that they can elicit.

Toward the end of the immersion process, all of us students went through a process where we discovered how the camera saw us, so that we could best market ourselves. For example, the camera reads me as "sharp and dangerous." Though I think of myself as warm and friendly and open—and though that is often how people relate to me in person—on camera, the angularity of my face and the confidence I exude reads as "sharp and dangerous." I pursued this "angle" and went to a hairdresser and simply said, "I need hair that makes me look sharp and dangerous." The result is recorded in the last photo of the series shown in Chapter 2 and continues to be the image I take into auditions. Learning to act, and seeing people's responses to me, made me more attuned to how I impact the world, simply by moving through it as a visual body. This is a major shift that occurred in my awareness.

Changes in My Personal Life

During my arts immersion, I ended my partnership with a man that I had been seeing. Several dreams and intuitions, to which I was paying particular attention, enabled me to see the lack of integrity in the situation. I recognized the relationship as a huge lesson for me in trusting my "horse sense" and the revelations of the dreams encouraged me to end it.

Through my work in class, on the play, and on the movies, I realized how isolated I had become after working for 10 years in private practice. I now consciously choose to connect with friends, people in the community in which I live, and in the creative community. I continue to hold my family as a priority in my life and have watched my relationship with my daughter grow through my involvement in creative work.

My family also expanded during the final stages of the immersion process with the addition of a golden retriever, "Angel." She had been a seeing-eye dog and needed a home to retire. On the day that I was considering whether to adopt her or not, and on which I had asked to be given messages from the Universe regarding which way to go, I had a synchronistic event at school—I was given the part of a blind lady to play. Angel now contributes her support and guidance along with my little Jack Russell, Nikki.

These changes that happened in my life were ones that I had affirmed and intended to draw into reality. That is, I affirmed that I have a great network of people and support around me.

Inner Transformations

Many of the changes I experienced took place in my inner world and included shifts in my beliefs and perceptions, as well as strengthening of my self-esteem. A deepened capacity to love was one of the most important changes that I experienced. It is also the most difficult to describe. It is a sensation of the heart that is deeper and lower in my body. It includes an increased ability to see others as parts of myself and an increased ability to forgive others and myself. It includes a commitment to making choices that align with integrity, joy, love, peace, and harmony, and feeling the results as I look around at my beautiful, warm, loving life.

I fought hard for this feeling during the course of my immersion. Daily, and it seemed constantly, I fought with the parts of myself that were impatient, angry, jealous, and judgmental. I felt like I was literally wrestling a dragon as I struggled with these "dark" feelings, using thought-stopping techniques, affirmations, and intentions in my head to realign myself with feelings of love, joy, and peace.

I must admit that, looking back, most days at school, I felt like I lost the battle to the dark parts of myself. When I remember my feelings then, I can only replace them with kinder, more patient, loving, peaceful, and non-judgemental feelings on an imaginal level now. I imagine it "as if" I held these feelings then, as if it happened then, and hope that the Universe receives this intention in that direction of time. I continue to forgive myself for my inability to operate at a higher level while in the moment. I have faith in the implications of the new science's findings that it is simply an assumption that we can only change the future based on learning from the past and continue to experiment with changing the past with what I know now. I question, too, the assumption of linearity with regard to the process of time and how we create effects in our world. Part of me would like to imagine that the good thoughts that I now send to my classmates and teachers from that period of history can shift and rescind negative or toxic effects from any negative thoughts and feelings I may have created during those dark times.

I am now more easily able to reach out and connect with people, and when I do, I feel our connections more deeply. Sometimes I catch myself when I am sitting, driving for example. I begin to notice that I am simply content and at peace, feeling gratitude and love in an almost palpable way coming from my heart and extending outwards. I have caught myself reviewing everyone I know and sending them love in a beam of light. This is not to say that I hadn't loved before, but I never did these kinds of things or felt this kind of intensity.

Working closely with Spirit for nine months during the immersion also gave me an increased knowing of the interconnectivity of life and my role in it. This increased awareness helps me pay closer attention to my dreams, intuition, body, and "messages" from other illogical, irrational places. I am more able to receive these messages, trust them, and act on them if necessary. With this increased awareness of interconnectivity comes an increased feeling of responsibility for every thought, image, feeling, and action that comes through me into the Universe. The heightened awareness of connection with Spirit gives me a feeling of safety and security, as though I am being cared for. The many synchronistic events that I experienced have especially solidified this feeling. I was able to recognize messages from Spirit that left me with no doubt that I was being received, and which were provided to me as a direct result of my request.

I have also learned how to effectively stop my fear/anger thoughts, which gives me an increased ability to prevent full-blown fear/anger cycles from overtaking me. Through practice, this ability has become more and more effective. I can now assist in the creation of peace in my own mind. A key lesson I learned is the vital significance of forgiveness. I have been consciously practicing forgiveness of others and of myself to the best of my abilities. The result has been a more accepting attitude of the full range of my being.

New Kinds of Awareness

When I began my journey of transformation, I wrote, thought, and spoke about changing the worldview as if it happened in a linear way and as if it were yet to happen. I now understand that "it" is already here and always has been here. It is a perspective and way of thinking about the world and the Universe that has always been accessible.

In my earlier writings, I spoke of the change of paradigm being one of moving from a materialistic worldview to a more spiritual worldview.

I now understand this to be inaccurate because this way of thinking still separates the physical from the spiritual. From my new perspective, the physical is what is generated, or created from the non-physical realm of creative energy. The new worldview includes the oneness of the physical and spiritual.

I now understand myself to be a vibrational being in a vibrational Universe. This gives me a whole new perspective on what it is to be human and allows me to see the world differently. I have thus shifted my perspective on "aliens." During my time of immersion, the metaphor of "aliens" challenged my beliefs about the "reality" of the Universe. I tell the full story in **Creative Inspiration VII**, "'Aliens' to Dinner." After allowing for the very real possibility that "aliens" existed, I also opened myself to the desire to make contact. It was synchronistic when, at the end of my studies at New Image College of Fine Arts, a teacher told me that some of my classmates actually believed that I was an alien.

Since then, my perspective has shifted to the point of simply seeing and understanding "aliens" to be vibrational experiences of consciousness along an infinite rainbow of frequencies. I have personally substituted the word "alien" with the word "being" in my vocabulary, because it eliminates the experience of fear and opens me to an experience of wonder and awe at the infinite variety of beings I can come to know. I understand these beings to be of the same ultimate Creative Source as us. Rather than picturing them as from another universe, I picture them as beings of a particular vibrational frequency still within our realms of Universe, because, after all, they are in our universe and experience, are they not? So, rather than thinking in terms of "alien encounters," I now consider such experiences to be with beings of different vibrational frequencies and different worldviews, not unlike the differences between myself and a person growing up in a culture and country totally foreign to me. I have developed a passion to become fluent in the language of Spirit, so I can develop my capacity to live continually in a state of conscious contact with a whole spectrum of beings who want the best for me.

I have really begun to know that I am the individualized expression of a Source of infinite power and love. I know, too, that my commitment to Joy and Love, and to being a person of integrity—along with my daily consciousness of redirecting my thoughts to these levels—puts me in conscious control of creating a life of freedom, joy, and love. I have realized the significance of my every thought, feeling, and behavior, and the impact that I have on the Universe by coming to understand my connection to Source and everything physical and non-physical. At the beginning of my immersion, I had a shift in realization that it was not other people that I had to change or impact. Rather the core of the change had to be myself. This realization has only deepened as time and experience have gone by.

More than ever, I understand that I have the power to change myself and my reality, because I am connected to Source and, through Source, to all that is. In being the change that I want to see in the world (as Gandhi recommended), my world changes and I affect all that is. I see my role more now as an agent of *inspiration* rather than as an agent of change. I inspire through my very presence and *being* in the world, through maintaining my connection to feelings of high vibrational frequency to the very best of my ability.

My Morning Pages show that I have shifted away from a focus on the material to a greater closeness with the spiritual. In my early writings, many of my intentions and visualizations focused on gaining money and material goods, whereas in my later writings the focus changed to intentions to connect more deeply with Spirit and to recognize Spirit as the Source. In my later writings there is an increase in my personal relationship with my "Senior Partner." My intentions reflect a desire to co-create days where I increase awareness, understanding, and knowledge of this Inner Presence. Over the course of my journaling, there was a decrease in intentions connected with self-importance and an increase in intention directed to choosing to be in alignment with Spirit. The writings reflect a release of pride and an increase in degree of humility. There is also an increase in sensitivity to the oneness in the Universe and a resulting change in my behaviors, especially in letting go of anxiety, and placing confidence in the Divine Consciousness that I am.

Regarding Choice and Ethics

This is a crucial time in Earth's history where great change is occurring. Our new understanding of the way the Universe works indicates that the choices of each individual person are crucial in determining the direction of the shifts in consciousness. These choices involve not only people's actions but, more importantly, the very thoughts and beliefs that they choose to entertain. We can channel our energies in the direction of higher vibrational frequencies, such as love, joy, and peace—which are in line with Source Energy—or we can choose such lower vibrational frequencies as fear, anger, and grief. The idea that we can choose our thoughts and emotions, to consciously work with a universal force to co-create reality, is becoming mainstream. With this awareness comes the capacity to consciously choose our future.

Choice can be in either direction, negative or positive. The forces of the Universe have no judgment. It is up to the individual and then the collective to choose belief systems, thoughts, and emotions. This implies the need for strong ethical training in order to guide individual choices toward the good, towards creation. It also implies the need for strong leaders who can guide the general population in the direction of good, and who can teach the methods to make the necessary changes and support people as they apply these changes in their lives.

In his lecture series, Dr. David Hawkins (2002, 2003) states that currently in the United States, over 50 percent of the population lies below the level of integrity. He notes that it is the 20 percent of individuals living in the realms of consciousness vibrating at frequencies of over 200 that maintain the balance in the world. This is important to realize, because as individuals become aware of their power to co-create reality, and then actually make positive choices in the direction of integrity, more and more leaders will move over the threshold of integrity. As this happens, individuals below the level of integrity will automatically be raised by the power of the collective. Dr. David Hawkins (2002) described this phenomenon as being like the ocean. As more people become aware of their personal power and then make the daily small choices to align with Source Energy, the collective ocean of consciousness rises, lifting up everyone and everything in it.

The crucial importance of making choices for the good and the need for responsibility must be communicated quickly and easily. The performing arts can greatly contribute toward inspiring these shifts in a positive direction and lifting people to these places. But to do so effectively, artists need to understand their role in the world. What I discovered in acting school was that actors train themselves to move into all the levels of consciousness in order to access their emotions so that they can bring truth into imaginary circumstances. They create reality through the use of intention; they move through energy fields of anger, joy, awe, and so on—until it feels real. Actors are modern-day shamans. They use the exact same tools as shamans to co-create reality: they take people—their audience—on journeys of emotions, journeys through levels of consciousness. They have the power to move people to levels resonating beyond reason and give them an experience of life at these levels. This is a process akin to those described in the literature of consciousness studies and the new science. This is a process that could be used in the reality of "real life" to create truth.

What I learned in acting school is that actors are some of the bravest people in the world. They train themselves to access some of the darkest vibrational energy of human beings. They willingly move to, and sustain, realms of emotions in their physical being, many of which are known to impact negatively on a cellular level. I often wondered about the implications at a soul or karmic level of an actor willingly connecting to very dark states of consciousness and sustaining that connection for any length of time.

I learned that when actors are good at what they do and connect with their own emotions, they elicit feelings from their audience. They take the audience on a journey with them. This is a powerful role. The actor has learned the power of transporting people into various states of consciousness, and we know that the feeling is the prayer or the vibration that attracts realities. I had one instructor brush off the educational and inspirational role that the performing arts play. He reminded everyone that what actors do is simply "entertainment." What he failed to see, from my perspective, is that even "entertainment"—stories put out with no intention to educate or inspire—move and shift people through levels of emotions that bring realities into being.

During my immersion, I found a group of youth who did not understand how sacred their work was. I found a need for training the young artists to value themselves and what they were doing. I felt a need to empower young artists. I saw an imperative to challenge a majority of these young artists regarding their motivation for being actors. I discovered that a majority of my classmates were being motivated by fame or money, an image often connected to life in film. I saw a need to open their eyes to higher motivations.

I observed a group of artists largely unaware of the impact of their work. I saw a need for some ethical discussion regarding the kind of projects people would agree to be in, considering the fact that the stories that they brought to life were eliciting emotions in the audience that were attracting particular realities in society. Did we as a group of artists want to continue being in films that elicit feelings of hate, anger, and fear? If we were made aware of how these emotions in people create certain realities on the world stage, would we at least stop and consider the implications of our work? And would the single act of becoming more aware change what we do and how we do it? I believe that it would.

There is a great need for unity among performing artists. What I experienced was a culture of competition: artists competing and comparing themselves to others, talking negatively of others, showing jealousy, and engaging in backbiting. Even in the larger culture, it is a world of competition—competing for work at auditions, competing to see who has the best film, who is the best student. On an even grander scale, in the award system of Hollywood, people are competing for Best Film, Best Actress, Best On-Screen Kiss, and so forth. Yet, in the arena of creativity, every creation is unique, with merit and worth of its own accord. People who write about creativity, and how best to foster its power, tell of the importance of acceptance, support, and collective groups of artists who pop each other into new realities. Yet, in my experience, such true community has been difficult to find. More frequently, there may be a façade of community underlined by a competitive spirit. Here is something that performing artists would do well to re-imagine. To moderate the milieu of competition would open the way for members of the performing arts community to take their place as world leaders alongside the politicians, scientists, and spiritual leaders.

What is most important for actors—indeed for society at large—to understand is the crossover between performance art and reality: that is, all of the tools that really great actors use to create various realities for us in performances are tools that we as humans can adopt to create realities for ourselves in "real life." The key is in being aware of the possibilities of doing so and then making conscious choices about what you want—being very careful what you ask for, because you just might get it. The connection between performance and reality brings a very different level of meaning to ideas about the relationship of art and life.

For me the best response to the question, "How does one change the world through the arts?" is to transform myself. I can change what I have control over: my own thoughts and perceptions. I can also work with the arts as a teacher, to educate and empower people to change their thoughts and feelings; to support them as they take the first steps in doing so; to tell them stories of how people do it; and to incorporate knowledge about vibrational frequencies into the way that the stories are told, through music, movement, and aesthetics.

In working to change the world by teaching through the arts, I am still learning about myself and what it is that I need to know. In this, I am true to the spirit of Gandhi's words: "You must be the change you wish to see in the world." As a teacher, as an artist, it becomes imperative to live as an example of the belief systems of the new worldview. I consider teaching the new worldview to be a sacred endeavor—learning about the nature of Source, or Creative Energy, itself and then sharing this with the world. Because I am an individual expression of Source Energy, I am Source Energy's ambassador of sorts.

This thread also weaves into what I learned a good performer does in order to engage the audience. I always thought that as a performer I was to pour my energy forth into the audience in order to bring them on the journey with me. My voice teacher, Sandra, was quick to pick this up and correct me. She informed me that what I needed to do as a performer was stay inside my body and my head and ensure that I really go through the journey on the inner realm to the greatest depths possible. My energy is then much stronger, as is my voice. She demonstrated the difference between projecting one's energy and voice versus containing it inside. Keeping my energy as an inner process increased the strength, volume, and projection of my voice. I have learned that in staying with my own journey inside, my energy reaches the audience and they can decide to take the journey with me—or not—and that is how the magic happens.

The Power of Thoughts

One of the main principles I have learned in my studies of consciousness is that thoughts are very powerful, they do have substance, and they impact the environment. I have also discovered that whatever you focus your attention on is what will be amplified. These two principles combined mean that I create my own reality by what I choose to pay attention to. For example, when I was doing the play, *Balm in Gilead*, the majority of my thoughts were negative, depressed, sad, and angry. Some of this negativity I consciously generated, particularly as I intentionally moved into the consciousness of my character, Billie, and imagined interacting with people in a skid row café.

I wanted the cause of some of my negative thoughts to be outside of me. I wanted these feelings to be the result of other cast members being absent, coming late, or coming unprepared—factors that seemed outside of my control. At the same time, I knew that I could choose to control my reactions to these behaviors. Despite my best efforts, I found myself continually sliding into being angry and sad in response to these behaviors. I noticed that prayer was my best stronghold against the avalanche of judging and the angry thoughts that I found myself entertaining about my fellow cast members. I amplified the Mother Teresa part of Billie's character and prayed on two levels—as Billie, for my fellow actors in character as "junkies, pimps, and whores," and as Duanita, for myself and my fellow students who, I could see, were falling deeper and deeper into creative blocks, resistance, and shadow aspects of themselves. Even so, I saw that prayer at all these levels was ineffective in keeping me out of the cesspool of negativity, judgment, blame, and criticism.

Sometimes I had moments of clarity, compassion, and even forgiveness for my fellow classmates and myself, and I wondered how much the depressing content of the play was affecting us as people. I also questioned how much of the absenteeism, lateness, and lack of preparation was self-sabotaging behavior, possibly symptomatic of creative blocks. After all, we were being asked to enter a play that dealt with very dark issues and which generated feelings of hopelessness, helplessness, and despair.

I knew that the level of consciousness that we were asked to enter was one of the lowest identified in Dr. Hawkin's Map of Consciousness. I was feeling great resistance toward immersing myself in these feelings, and I wondered whether this was also happening for my classmates, possibly unconsciously. I had to work hard to find a point of connection and then to give life to my character, even knowing full well what I was entering. What would it have felt like if I did not know the regions into which I was going? I thought that it would surely be easy to get lost.

I then took the perspective of all the theory I had read and applied the principles to my experience. First, I had to make the statement that I was totally responsible for everything that happened. I took full responsibility for creating the reality I lived through. I took full responsibility for the thoughts I had and the choices I made. Had I created all of the unprofessional behavior in my fellow actors? It seemed a stretch, yet I was thinking very negative thoughts about them, despite my best efforts to hold these at bay. Was my focus on the negative amplifying it and giving it a reality?

On reflection, I see that I could have made very different choices. I could have applauded them when they did come on time. I could have reached out to them individually to see if they were being triggered by the material. I could have asked if I could help in any way. I could have put more emphasis on changing the place to which my thoughts continued to sink.

But instead of making these choices, I chose to sit quietly in my chair as Billie. I was angry and focused on everything that they did wrong. I used these facts as fuel for continuing to remain angry and depressed and hopeless—and, in some bizarre way, to feel better than all of them. They were all worthless, no good. I was the hard worker, the one who took care of everything, who was "better than" them. The worlds between my "character" and my character blurred. Consumed as I was by self-righteousness, I was incapable of insight about my behavior both as Billie and as Duanita. Later, just asking the question—about how and why I created this reality—brought about the insight that I constructed a world where I could feel superior and aloof and "take care of" them in a martyr kind of way.

These insights lead me to a question that was sparked for me throughout the course of my training. Do actresses "create" or draw to them roles that are exactly what they need at the time to learn life lessons about aspects of themselves? For example, did I attract the play *Balm in Gilead* and the character Billie because of my inner self-sacrificing, judging, self-righteous martyr that I needed to deal with? And if so, why did that particular part materialize at this particular point in my life?

As I went through all of the courses working with script after script, role after role, and watching my colleagues, I was always amazed at the roles we would get and how they usually mirrored some issue that was going on in our personal lives. For example, the foreign student got assigned the role of a killer by an instructor who had no idea about his history in the army of his country of origin. The females in the class who had histories of sexual abuse were typically the ones assigned the roles of sexual abuse victims. A scene about an abortion came up for the student who had privately undergone one, and instructors unwittingly gave the druggy roles to the people experimenting with drugs. And invariably, the prima donna roles went to the females in class who lived that reality, with rich boyfriends and people around them who took care of them and put up with their volatile moods. Another thing that amazed me was that usually the alignment of actor and role would be obvious to everyone in the class—except the chosen actor. Looking back, I cannot help but question what would have happened if, through the onslaught of negativity, I had held to my original view of my classmates as young, creative beings doing the very best that they could, faced with an extremely intense program of study. What if I had continued to see the negative, unprofessional behaviors simply as creative blocks? What if I had acted on my impulse to help them through these blocks? What if I had stood up to the teacher who told me to back down when I brought up my concerns; who told me that they had much more experience in the field of acting than I did; who told me that there had been a way to teach acting that had been established for centuries? Would Socks still be alive today if I had chosen to speak up, act, or work harder to change my thoughts?

The Power of Actions

During the immersion I came up with dozens of rationalizations for refraining from helping fellow students. Eventually I convinced myself to do nothing except slide deeper and deeper into anger, resentment, bitterness, unforgivingness, and judgment. But what if I had done something and even one person had changed perspective? What if even more did? What if so many cast members changed their perspectives and began looking at the unprofessional behaviors as creative blocks that we actually could discuss them? Things might have been very different.

My awareness of another way of looking at what was going on was not enough. I was also required to act, and I chose to remain immersed in the negativity rather than pull out with positive action. Though it is no excuse, I can understand, have empathy for, and forgive myself for the path that I did take. In fact, I am at least grateful that even with everything going on, I was able to curtail certain behaviors like negative gossip about other people and huge angry fights with colleagues—behaviors that were happening with others. I was doing the best I could with what I knew as a beginning actor who was working with enormously challenging material and an extremely challenging character.

I can only hope that as I gain experience as an actress I am more easily able to maintain my "Self" in a state of love, compassion, and insight. I am hoping that it becomes easier and easier for me to quickly shift out of the anger/sadness/hopelessness states of consciousness that I am required as an actress to enter. I am hoping to be able to learn how to keep in better touch with myself instead of being swept away on a current of negativity. I am hoping to discover my courage to be brave and break out with positive thoughts and actions, no matter how impossible the context seems.

Where will the new skills I learned take me? And what are the implications of my playing a new role of "actress" and "artist" in the real world? We can only wait to see. My first venture into the world of performing will always help remind me of what a slippery slope it is when one is learning to shift to, and maintain, higher states of consciousness. The experience will be something I can return to in recollection, and which will enable me to have compassion for other humans making the shift in their own selves.

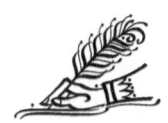

eleven
The Way Ahead

Agent of Inspiration

The more I thought about my recent journey through the arts and consciousness, the more I came to know that the journey would be ongoing—that the way ahead would be one with the place I had come from. I had been, and would strive to remain, an agent of inspiration for others.

After the first performance of *Emerging*, several audience members commented that they were moved and inspired by the presentation of my personal story about going through the initiation process at the college and what I was learning as a result. One 19-year-old audience member said that my story encouraged him to look at all the ways he was stopping himself by being too critical of himself. A woman in her 40s said, "It made me realize that I am not too old to start all over again in another career if I wanted to." Similarly, many people watching me go through the program reported being inspired by my mere presence and participation in the studies. Several of the students, for instance, would tell me that they would want to be like me when they reach my age—that is, still doing new things and having the courage to learn and change.

Others were inspired by the amount of work that I did as a student, particularly considering the fact that I also continued to run my business and keep my priorities as a single-parent mother devoted to her young daughter. An example of this occurred one day when several students had failed to do their homework for a singing class. During break, one of the students who had not done her homework said, "You know, there is just no excuse for it. If Duanita can finish hers with everything else that she has to do in her life, surely I can finish mine." Toward the end of the program, one of the teachers said to me, "You know, in all the while I have been teaching you, I can say with certainty that never have you come to class unprepared. You are a great role model for everyone."

My 11-year-old daughter's observation that I was my classmate's "Guardian Angel" also attests to the inspirational role I played, simply by participating in this study. She made this comment to me on the ride home from my performance of *Emerging*. She had been watching my interactions with my classmates throughout the evening very carefully, without my awareness. She had seen one fellow student come up to me for support because her boyfriend just broke up with her, another fellow student come up to me for encouragement because her family had failed to show up for the performance, and others come up to me for peer support before going on. When I began to question what on earth I was doing in the program, questioning whether I had made a mistake, my daughter began recounting what she had seen that evening and told me that I was there because I was a Guardian Angel for the other students, showing them that it could be done, and convincing them that they could do it. Her words impacted me deeply.

I began to watch my daughter's reactions to my initiation experience and realized that the mere fact of my going through the program was affecting our relationship in a positive transformational way. For example, she got to see me in a different role from the usual "Mother." She saw me as a student—and as a student at 45 years of age. I still wonder what impact her memories of this time will have when she reaches this age. I do know how thrilled she was to meet all my fellow classmates. I am an introverted person who has about five really close friends, most of whom live in other countries. My daughter, as a result, rarely sees me with my friends. She commented on this dimension of my experience throughout and, every night before bedtime, she would want to hear stories of how each of my classmates was doing.

These daily bedtime stories are very important to mention because, as a therapist, I was never free to tell her, or anyone else, the actual details of what I did every day. As a student, I was no longer bound by confidentiality to the same extent. I began to share my life with her in a whole new way.

She could now get to know my world, the characters in it, and me. As a result, our relationship changed and deepened, especially in my ability to laugh, joke around, and be silly with her.

My daughter connected to my classmates and to several of my teachers. She was excited to get autographs from them after performances. She was inspired to get them Christmas and graduation presents and cards. She also ensured that she had their contact in-formation and continues email and MSN contact with them to this day, independent of me.

I regard these actions as indicators of the excitement and inspiration she felt as a result of my journey. Recently at her school they were asked to look at career choices and she began searching the area of fine arts. Though she is naturally inclined in this way, I found myself wondering what kind of effect her experience with the people in my program, and watching me go through the program, might have on her future career decisions.

During and after my immersion, I used what I had learned to inspire my clients and students. For example, in several courses, I have made the "Co-Create Your Day" an assignment and observed several students experience life transformations. One man learned how to follow synchronistic happenings, and these events buoyed him up through a period when he had given up on a dream of his. He had applied for a scholarship for some study travel and had been placed as an alternative scholar who would go if the winner was in some way unable to. The synchronicities allowed him to remain hopeful and to continue to do his work "as if" he had won the award. Several days before the award winner was to leave, my student was called. The formal winner was unable to make the journey and my student was asked to take his place. My student's dream came true.

I have seen many other clients educate themselves and begin applying such methods as the Co-Creating Your Day Journaling process. I have watched their perspectives shift, their quality of life improve, their faith and hope restored. A husband who wanted to leave his wife began practicing extending love to her and, as a result, found a renewed interest in staying. I have seen it help people as they moved through a transitional phase in life, through divorce or career change. I have seen it lift people out of depressed places to a place of hope—in particular, clients who asked for, and then received, big "signs" that left them with no doubt that they were having an impact at a subatomic level.

Embracing the Sacred, Partnering with Spirit

In the beginning I set forth on my journey with the assumption that all things are sacred. And I resolved to embrace the Sacred by partnering with Spirit at every step of the way.

To inspire others to a reality based on love, kindness, harmony, and a realization of the sacredness and interconnectedness of all, I had to deeply know that place and live from it. First of all, in order to help facilitate the shift in worldview at this point in history, I needed to learn the language of Spirit. I had never even thought about the language of Spirit as an area of study when I began this book. From my perspective now, I really believe that it is crucial to the shift to a spiritual worldview to know how to communicate with a consciousness that is abstract, beyond human form, and beyond human language. By asking Spirit to communicate with me on a daily basis, I began to know the ways in which this happens. In order for me to recognize when Spirit was honoring my request and communicating with me, I had to learn to pay more attention to such higher faculties as intuition, telepathy, and psychic awareness. Then, even more importantly, I had to learn to trust them. I had to learn to trust my experiences that often were out of step with what I had learned were the laws of the world.

My most powerful lesson was learning how to listen to messages from Spirit when they came through my intuition and/or my body. Though I always seemed to recognize these as messages from Spirit, it often took a powerful lesson to help me trust these messages when they came. In the end, because I learned to embrace the realm of the intuitive, I was able at last to break free from the unhealthy relationship that had kept me down for too long. I tell the story as **Creative Inspiration VIII**, "Trusting Horse Sense."

It was easier for me to see and trust messages from Spirit that came through animals. In these cases, however, the meaning of the message was often difficult to decipher. I have recorded one of the most powerful experiences of this kind that occurred just after I had graduated from the fine arts program. You can read about it in its entirety in **Creative Inspiration IX**, "Signs."

Because I had worked with my dreams for 20 years, I was also comfortable with this method of communication with Spirit. Just as with so many of Spirit's messages, however, I often was required to simply live with knowing that Spirit was communicating with me via my dreams and that I was unable to fully understand.

Synchronicities were often the easiest way for me to spot a communication from the Universe. I have learned to pay attention and follow them because when I do, inevitably I am led in a direction of value. So, for example, I was "led" to many of the books and resources I studied during the course of writing this book. Sometimes they would fall off a shelf when I was in a bookstore, or a book would be given to me, and/or several people in succession would recommend that I look at something. Following the lead of these occurrences always gave me the feeling that I was "on track."

It is this feeling of deep purpose that has been the best part of partnering with Spirit. Whenever I received a message from Spirit, no matter the form, no matter even whether I understood it or not, it was like undeniable confirmation of the larger, responsive, conscious Universe that I lived in. After such a message, there was no question about the reality of oneness or interconnectedness. There were no longer principles of a worldview I *believed* to be true—but principles of a worldview I knew to be true—unshakably true. And it did not matter whether anyone believed me or not. I knew. Without actually partnering with Spirit and experiencing this knowing, I would have remained at the level of only believing.

Whether through signs, synchronicities, or intuitive answers to my questions, my faith was always enriched after I experienced Spirit in these ways. And inevitably, there was an increase in my energy level. As I received the messages from Spirit, I was "inspired," filled with Spirit. This energy kept me going when I felt lost or when I had a lot of work to do. It kept me connected to, and interested in, writing this book. This energy buoyed me up when I was discouraged and kept me going when I was tired. It greatly assisted me in deepening my appreciation for the value of studying shifts in consciousness via the arts. With each message from the Universe, or Spirit, I desired all the more to learn how to communicate more effectively and pass on the knowledge to others.

The language of Spirit is important to begin showing to the world via films, television, and stage plays. By seeing examples of this language, people may in their own lives become aware of how Spirit is communicating with them. In *Emerging* I told the audience how I had followed a dream and synchronicities to lead me to study in the area of acting. During class many months later, one of my classmates quipped that he wished he would have a dream like me that would just show him the way. His interest had obviously been caught and, even months later, he was still expressing this wish. And such expression is one of the first steps in turning a desire into actual experience.

I next needed to cultivate flexibility and the ability to surrender. After receiving a message from Spirit, I needed to follow the lead given—even if I did not understand it. Sometimes this would be a very small thing, like a little voice telling me to turn a corner while driving. I often found myself resisting following these nudges from Spirit, talking myself out of doing as I was asked, giving all kinds of reasons why I did not need to. As time went on, though, I learned to surrender more and more to the intention of Spirit—however imperfect my understanding of it might be. When I do so, things often go in ways I would never have planned.

For example, as I was writing this book one night just before bedtime, I mulled over the question, "How has partnering with Spirit made a difference in what I learned on my journey?" I woke up at 3:00 a.m. filled with energy, so I decided to begin writing. It was a Sunday, a day that I usually reserve for family only, no work. A client that week had reminded me that it was actually one of the Ten Commandments to keep one day during the week for rest. But I felt like I wanted to write and went to work on my Morning Pages. I was just about to write this section of the book when my daughter came to me with a disturbing dream. "I had a bad dream, Mama. It doesn't seem like a bad dream but it really was. I dreamt that you had to work from 5 in the morning until 11 at night and that we couldn't go to my singing or dancing today. It was awful."

Her dream stopped me in my tracks. It seemed a clear message from Spirit, reminding me to keep my family a priority over my career and to ensure that I kept at least one day a week sacred, a day where no work is done. If I had sunk into my writing, I would have been preoccupied for the duration of the day, not really present during my daughter's singing and dancing. Even if I had attended in person, my mind would have failed to be present. I quickly chose to change my plan to write through the night and went to lie down with my daughter, grateful that Spirit was able to clearly and effectively realign me with one of my original intentions: "family always comes before career."

My willingness to alter plans, listen, and surrender to Spirit came from being continually faced with choices to follow Spirit's bidding or not. Though I could easily say that I would follow Spirit's intentions, it was quite a different thing to actually have to do it—to make the choices and take the actions that sometimes were so opposite to what I was inclined to do. This surrendering and following is rather like my experience as a dancing partner in Argentine tango. In order to follow when I dance, I must feel the lead and then choose to surrender and respond to it. The degree to which I can do it, and we can move as one, depends on how much I trust my partner. This is exactly the same with Spirit. The more we communicate and the more I trust, the easier it is to follow, sometimes even with my eyes closed. And sometimes, just as in dance, we align so completely that I have the experience of being one with Spirit. It is in such moments that a door opens to an experience beyond words—an experience that could never have happened to me if I had failed to partner with Spirit. Partnering with Spirit has allowed me to gain knowledge of realities at very high levels of consciousness.

Partnering with Spirit also acted as a mirror for me personally, showing me areas of myself that needed to be aligned with higher vibrational energies. This was very painful for me, because it required that I take personal responsibility for everything I disliked in my reality, find these very qualities in myself, and make some changes. For example, one personal area that required attention was my tendency to judge others and to get angry quickly. I look back over the class dynamics during the immersion, and I shudder at the way I behaved and the inner monologue that went on inside me. I was in the grips of an internal struggle between judgment, criticism, and negativity on one side and loving, acceptance, praise, and positivity on the other.

It was an opportunity for these qualities in myself to be brought to light and for me to work with thought-stopping in order to move to more positive levels. I certainly have never felt that I mastered all of these personal challenges that Spirit revealed for me; however, I do feel that I did the very best that I could with what I knew at the time. This knowledge of my areas of personal weakness and the tremendous effort and commitment it takes to shift them could only have been gained by partnering with Spirit in a reflective way. Such knowledge makes a difference in my ability to be an effective agent of inspiration, and it gives me empathy with the conflicts other people might go through when they choose to lift some of their lower energies above the level of integrity.

There was an especially marvellous effect of partnering with Spirit. While my journey of transformation required total involvement—with serious time and energy commitments on both personal and professional levels—I felt so free. My journey was an adventure, each moment leading to another. I could not wait to see what would happen next.

Partnering with Spirit has brought meaning and change into my life. I know that what I write of and the transformations that occurred are true. I may never know whether or not I was actually working with consciousness. I may never know whether these same changes might have happened anyway for me as a result of other factors. Yet I have a deep knowing that my story as I relate it is true and trans-formative for me, and for others. It is this truth that gives it validity for me.

I have been changed. I have seen others change. I wonder about the changes yet to come through the stories I created in class and those I have recounted here. Now, you see, all that has happened came about because I made my journey in partnership with Spirit. As the partnership continues, I wonder what stories I have yet to tell with my newly acquired acting skills and my knowledge of the creative arenas of film, television, and stage. And what transformations are yet to manifest?

I became—and am still becoming—the change that I wish to see in the world. This is where I came from and the way that lies ahead. This is oneness—this is truth. This is embracing the Sacred.

Just Have Faith

Albert Einstein once remarked that he would prefer to think of a concrete universe—a choice that left his work calibrating on the upper edge of reason, never making the leap of faith into the higher realms. I can only look forward to the day when the great ones among us more readily make the leap of faith necessary to attain the levels of spirituality. We do not have to keep taking centuries to validate scientifically what is already apparent through other ways of knowing.

As I complete this book, I am reminded of words my mother often spoke to me. My mother is a woman who spent her life devoted to her family. She has a quiet wisdom that comes from being a woman of strong faith. She never had the opportunity to have much formal education after high school. Though she is tremendously proud of my academic achievements, she often hesitates to ask me about what I am doing and it is rarely part of our conversations.

One day, however, I had just arrived home from attending a conference where some of the consciousness leaders of our time were speaking. My mom had flown out to our home to take care of my daughter for me. As we were sitting on the couch, she asked me, "So what exactly was this conference about?" Her question surprised me and I took a moment to answer in a way she could fully understand. "Well," I responded, "really what it was about is people giving scientific evidence that prayer works, that angels exist, and that God is real." I was excited to be able to share and eagerly awaited her response, hoping to be able to tell her all the exciting information I had just learned.

"Well," she said, "I don't understand why they don't just have faith. Why do they need to prove these things?"

Her question stopped me in my tracks. I began to laugh—at myself. I realized that my mother had devoted her life to training me when I was a child in the art of having faith, a lesson that she had taught me well, because I still hold the faith of my childhood in my heart. I was also, however, the type of person who needed to understand with my head.

I'd had questions, and I had searched the world for teachers and read the words in books, looking for the answers. The irony was that, after actually finding the information that could confirm my beliefs, I had come full circle to find myself back at the beginning, at my roots. I realized that throughout my lifelong search for answers, for information—for "proof"—I had actually held the key all along. It was in the form of the gift my mother had given me as a child—the gift to "just have faith."

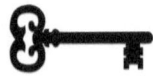

Creative Inspirations

I ~ Morning Pages

Note: The source for the concept of Morning Pages is Julia Cameron, *The Artist's Way* (1992). Morning Pages are three pages of longhand writing, strictly stream-of-consciousness—in other words, "brain drain," the purpose of which is to get rid of all the negative "stuff" that stands between you and your creativity.

Sample Excerpts

September 21, 2005

Today the characters are developed . . . their history . . . the atmosphere . . . the feeling . . . and it all happens quickly and easily . . . It is a process I will use many, many times in my life as an actor and writer . . . so I do it . . . letting God's voice through always.

September 25, 2005

Today God—let's have a really productive day together, okay? We focus on my creative project. We write the script—the best that we can do . . . and we go look for a dress/shoes . . . and we also get some new material and make the mask. It is really coming together. I am so grateful.

September 20, 2005

Today I make my choices in alignment with truth. The field I am in is a consequence of my choice. I choose to be free. I choose to be beautiful. I choose to never work too hard. I choose to play and be happy. I choose to really be there for my daughter and to spend lots of time with her every day.

I resolve myself to making good choices everyday—healthy choices. I bring in a field of pure love into this household . . . into this family . . . which can be felt.

Yes . . . and today I watch as you give me the signs that you are there—responsive and responding . . . co-creating this with me—helping me to bring in these fields. I love it when you arrange for something to happen and it so surprises me, and it leaves me no doubt that you are there—responding.

II ~ "Sharing Miracles," by Duanita Gaye

Source: "A Favorite Collage Activity," by Julia Cameron (1992)

It was 1994. I was diligently working my way through *The Artist's Way: A Spiritual Path to Creativity*, by Julia Cameron (1992). I am forever picking up interesting books and doing the programs myself to see what happens. As a therapist, I think that it is always a good idea for me to first do any art activities/directives that I might want to do with clients/students.

I did the collage she recommends, in which I put images of my "dreams" into a magic circle. I then posted the image in a place where I would see it daily. At the time I did this, I was very pregnant and very broke. My nesting instincts had moved me to buy a condo and make preparations for the baby. There was no extra money to spend on my dreams.

Yet, as life would have it, this is exactly when I began to have nighttime dreams—dreams of being back in Hawaii. I had done my first Master's in Clinical Social Work and Research at the University of Hawaii, and it had been 10 years since I had been back. I had been doing my dream work for 15 years prior and had really come to learn the importance of sometimes literally living my dreams.

So here come the dreams of Hawaii. The dreams were so real that I felt like I was there. But . . . How could I go? I was pregnant and had no money.

I had been doing Cameron's course long enough to quickly put away the creative block that is one of the most commonly used, according to Cameron—the block of saying "I have no money." Instead, I practiced simply being open to my images and saying, "How do I go to Hawaii?"

I decided to honor my dreams the best way I could. I went to travel agencies, picked up some travel brochures on Hawaii, and proceeded to cut and paste my dream images into reality—the reality of the mandala-shaped collage. In my collage I felt myself at the beach—holding a small babe in my arms.

I put the collage up in a place where I could see it daily and I continued to move through life—through the summer and through the birth of a very beautiful daughter.

Then it was Christmastime and I bought a Christmas cloth. Now, I never buy Christmas cloths, and this one was particularly ugly. I chalked it up to hormones as I found myself in a long Christmas shopper line-up (another scene I actively avoid in my life), so that I could return the cloth.

So there I am, standing in a line-up, still leaking from every orifice after the birth, wondering what the heck I was doing there! Then I see a contest on the salesperson's desk: "Win a Trip for Two to Hawaii." My collage mandala of Hawaii, still on my wall, comes to my mind and I am moved to fill out the application. "You are waiting in line anyway," my inner voice says.

When I get to the front of the line-up and ask the woman where to drop off the contest form she tells me that the box is in the travel department. Oh my goodness! I have no energy. My shirt is wet with breast milk that has leaked beyond all the extra pads. I just want to go home.

My collage image comes back to me and my little voice kicks in: "Well, if you feel that it is too much effort to walk this form over there, lots of people probably feel the same way and your chances of winning will be higher."

I shake my head at the clarity of the voice and drag myself to the travel department to put the form in the box.

Two weeks later, I arrive home from work to discover that I had won the trip for two to Honolulu. Two months later, I was on the beach with my babe in my arms. I was reconnecting with old professors and fellow students. I was living the images from my collage and from my dreams.

So what is my point? It was crucial for me to honor my inner images and bring those images to this reality in the form of that mandala. That mandala of my hopes and wishes and the fact that I placed it in a spot where I was constantly reminding myself of their existence facilitated my ability to hold those images for a very long time. In the end, it was the power inherent in those images that gave me the strength to do the follow-through to bring them into concrete form and ultimately to bring my dreams into this "reality," so that I could live them.

When we live creatively, when we honor our images, hold them, express them . . . anything is possible. "Miracles" happen. We can easily envision the realities that we are to live.

III ~ An Article Inspired by *Emerging*

At 44 years of age, I realized the importance or value of aesthetics—working with line, shape, and color in order to evoke feelings. At the same time I was researching consciousness: the paradigm we are living in and the world crisis it is creating; the new paradigm that is slowly becoming a reality. My main question was "How?" How can we change the world consciousness to align with the new paradigm as quickly as possible?

I learned that the key is to help people to "feel," to give them an experience of the new reality. This brought me back to the arena of aesthetics. How could I work with line, shape, and color in order to provide people with an experience of the new paradigm and hopefully open the pathways for a breakthrough in human consciousness?

Because I am a professional art therapist, social worker, and instructor, I began to imagine learning about line, shape, and color in order to enhance my professional presentations. I quickly learned that aesthetics had been a blind spot for me throughout my life and career. I had been adamant that it be what I knew rather than how I looked that was important. Growing up through the tail end of the feminist movement even gave me a political righteousness to help me reinforce this belief.

It did not take much research to show me how wrong I was. When I came down from the academic, ivory tower-idealistic world I had been living in and entered the real world, the importance of aesthetics became very apparent. I was shocked to learn that as an educator, my audiences were sizing me up in less than three minutes based on what I looked like, not on what I said. I was even more shocked to realize that if I were to make an impact, I would have to learn more about beauty and the raw power of sex to "sell." I quickly realized that if I really wanted to make an impact on human consciousness at a global level, in order to induce the shift in world consciousness, working with aesthetics in a way that appealed to mass consciousness would be a far more powerful tool than writing yet another academic paper that would gather dust in a library somewhere and only be read by other academics.

Thus began my investigation into aesthetics. What could I learn about working with line, color, and form to evoke certain feelings that I could apply to my presentations to give them more impact? And where would I learn this?

A quick investigation into literature on aesthetics convinced me that I had been missing the boat for a long time. I began to see how my political views and my North American upbringing had left me blind to the value of working with beauty, sexuality, line, shape, and form. I realized that if I were to have maximum impact in the arena of consciousness I had to develop myself in this area and find a way to apply it.

At first I thought that I would simply do a makeover on myself—which I did. I took a foray into the world of modeling and went through an "Urban Renewal" program where I learned how to work with line, shape, and form as it applied to my visual image as a professional woman.

I went through a program with consultations on my hair, makeup, and wardrobe. Through a series of self-explorations we developed an image for me . . . an image we defined as "dramatically classic." This was my new style, to be reflected in my clothes, my attitude, my office, and my way of being in the world. It became an intention regarding my own personal aesthetic.

And it worked. Suddenly people were listening and paying attention to me in ways that had never happened before. For example, while waiting to leave a restaurant I decided to play with the way I stood, the way I held my feet. Within seconds I had two men stand up and offer me a seat. This had never happened before. At a presentation, the brooch that was added to a classic pantsuit for "drama" mesmerized some women and got complimented in the thank-you card they sent me. Most importantly through this process, I realized how much energy I had for years actually put into being invisible, attracting no attention, and especially no sexual attention to myself.

Further exploration into the arena of modeling led me to an interview at the New Image College of Fine Arts. While making the decision of whether or not to attend a full-time acting program, I had a dream that I was walking through a door onto a stage carrying a butterfly on my finger while at the same time I was watching myself (from just above my right shoulder). I took this dream as a sign that I needed to be onstage being witnessed at the same time as witnessing myself on stage. So I entered the school, trusting my dreams, trusting the Universe, and with the image of the butterfly to guide me.

Very shortly upon entering, I had another dream in which I was told to drop my "mask of sympathetic understanding." I knew what this meant. I simply did not know how deep the issue went.

I had created a "mask of sympathetic understanding" all of my life, beginning as a child. Until the dream came and I went through acting school, I had no real clear idea of how identified I had become with this persona.

It was a face I put on as a child in order to survive in a world that had no room for developing artists or creativity. It was the face I developed in a career as a therapist working in the trenches, day after day, hour after hour, hearing people's stories of pain, trauma, loss, sexual abuse, and violent households. It was a face I refined as an educator listening to my students. It was a face I never took off.

At acting school, as I explored characters and found my arena of characters within, I began to see how my "mask of sympathetic understanding" limited me. I was more than a therapist, more than the person who could listen and help.

At acting school I was challenged. In the first week I was told: "Be seen. Be heard." This immediately set off an inner conflict. All my life I was trained to "be a lady." If I let myself go that would be "boisterous." I learned to hide my inner energy . . . behind the "mask of sympathetic understanding."

Behind this mask I was never truly seen. I never shared anything about myself. I listened to others. I understood. I learned to hide.

The mask was an academic mask that I wore in my ivory tower. As an academic I very quickly disconnected my head from my body. My early training had taught me the vices of the body and never to trust the body.

Well, at acting school, suddenly I was told that my body was my tool. And therein, my adventure began . . . and my play *Emerging* captured it.

IV ~ Script for *Emerging*

Sings "Alleluia"

Remove your mask of sympathetic understanding.

Narrator

Great intro, huh? It was a dream of mine . . . an actual nighttime dream.

In the dream, I was watching myself from somewhere above my right shoulder. I watched as I moved from backstage through a door—onto a stage . . . front and center . . . into the lights . . . carrying a butterfly on my left hand.

I am a woman who has devoted my life to bringing my dream images into reality. (Hold up mask)

I have discovered that the trick is to get into relationship with the hints that the dream world gives me. Then it is about me having the courage, humility, and faith to follow the tiny clues from the dream, having absolutely no idea where they will lead me.

Following the image of the butterfly, I began to study beauty and aesthetics in a very PhD-ish, academic kind of way. My research led me, by chance, to an acting school . . . and there, a door opened . . . I walked through . . . (begin spinning round and round) . . . fell in a rabbit hole and found myself, to my utter amazement, in an acting class.

Acting Teacher

(Whistles "Fiddler on the Roof")

Welcome. Welcome. Welcome to acting school. Come everyone, come. Find your light. The very first thing you need to learn as an actor is that it is your responsibility to be seen and be heard. Remember, you are a gift to the world.

I am Maroosha . . . your voice and movement teacher . . . and in this class we practice to be seen and be heard.

The second thing we learn today is that as actors, our bodies are our tools. Now, let's warm up our lips, tongue and throat.

(Do the brrr, hmm, ahh . . . thing.) And now that we are warmed up, let's whistle. (Whistle . . . "Whenever I Feel Afraid")

Narrator

And it is from these very first words uttered by the acting teacher that my inner conflict began.

Luci

Be seen and be heard?! Is she kidding? That is the exact opposite of what I have been trained to do. I can't do that. My mask, my mask does not allow me to be seen or be heard. Maybe if I took it off . . . for just a moment. (She begins to take the mask off and whistle tentatively.)

Narrator

Well, even a slight thought of removing that mask of sympathetic understanding even just for a moment was enough to bring out an inner voice of mine, an inner character that I fondly refer to as Sister Marie.

Sister Marie

Luci, don't you dare remove that mask or listen to this woman. And get out of that light at once! And stand up straight for goodness sakes!

Luci, you are a therapist . . . not an actor. Your calling is to help people . . . to help people by being quiet and listening. It does not matter who you are, Luci. Your job is to help others . . . to always think of others before yourself.

Limelight, indeed. I mean really, Luci . . . look at her . . . listen to her whistling . . . you know that good girls never whistle . . . besides . . . there's a cross in the house.

Narrator

Oh, oh. I have always loved whistling. Even as a child I would risk the wrath of God and whistle in the house, even though I was told that it was a sin. Those words always bring out the rebel in me.

Bambii

(Whistles) No whistling because there is a cross in the house. What the hell does that mean anyway? Why are you so afraid of any expression of joy?

Sister Marie

(Crosses self) And who, pray tell, are you?

Bambii

Cesta, I am your worst nightmare. I'm Bambii. That's Bambii with two i's. (Laughs)

See . . . I live inside of Luci. Just like you, I am part of her, part of her dream life. Only, unlike you, I am the part of her that has the balls to really reveal myself . . . literally in fact. (Laughs)

And I am here, Cesta, to stop you. I am here to make sure that Luci can follow her dream through to the end. Luci needs to dance, laugh, sing, act . . . and whistle. She does need to be seen and be heard and to do that . . . she has to get rid of that mask.

Sister Marie

(Crosses herself)

Luci is a therapist, not an actor. She cannot just turn her back on her clients, her students, her healing abilities, her calling. She has obligations . . . responsibilities, not that you would understand that.

Luci has a brilliant mind . . . a superb heart. She has no need for beauty . . . even for her body.

Bambii

(Kicks)

Back off, Cesta. Why are you so determined to stop Luci from living in her body?

You have kept her invisible, hidden all these years in her little office . . . helping people . . . being the responsible one. Can't you for once just let her get out from behind her mask, be free, and have some fun?

Sister Marie

(Crossing herself)

Fun? You think that fulltime acting school would be fun for her? I mean, look around you. These students are teenagers, with flawless skin and no wrinkles . . . no sagging bodies . . . no gray hair . . . their whole lives ahead of them.

Luci is 45 years old. And she is simply not good enough to be an actor. She thinks her stories are great but they're not really. No one will want to hear them. Her dancing, her singing . . . her body . . . none of it is good enough.

Have fun? Change her profession now? At 45? It's illogical . . . irrational. She cannot just go out and chase her dreams . . . elusive butterflies. No, Luci is just fine as she is. There is no need for her to change.

Bambii

Luci is not fine. She is safe.

Luci . . . that mask may keep you safe . . . and it also keeps you hidden, unseen, and unheard. It has blinded you to your beauty and your freedom . . . both of which are there . . . if you would just come out . . . come out from behind that mask. Take a risk and bring the dream to reality.

Luci

Stop it! Stop it both of you! You are driving me crazy!

Bambii, Sister Marie! You know, you aren't so different. Yes, you are different . . . different parts of me . . . but we are all one. You both live in me . . . and I need both of you.

I am scared you know . . . really scared. I mean, can I actually do it? Can I actually perform . . . in front of people . . . show them what is really inside of me . . . reveal myself . . . be honest about who I really am?

I need both of you to help me. Bambii, you give me the courage to do what I need to do to follow my dream. And Sister Marie you give me the humility. It takes both humility and courage on the journey to truth. With both of you working together inside me, I can work with my whole being and bring this dream to life.

(Luci now sings "We all come from the Mother.")

Luci

I am seen and heard.

My body is my tool.

I am beautiful.

I am free.

Thank you.

END

V ~ Intentions for *Emerging*

1. I write plays that inspire people.

2. I write plays that change people's lives.

3. I write plays that calibrate in the levels of enlightenment.

4. I allow God's Will—God's Hand, God's ideas—to come through in this play.

5. I perform the play superbly—with grace, beauty, and skill.

6. I listen carefully to my intuition and the synchronicities that happen as the play takes form.

7. The work is God's work.

8. The work is a great piece of art.

9. The work is fun.

10. I am brilliant at creating a context within which to deliver Truth so that it is credible.

11. I am a brilliant, awesome, outstanding actress, dancer, and singer.

12. I am supported by other artists of high caliber.

13. The plays are seen—people want to see the plays and other people even want to perform them.

14. I form a theater company and I write wonderful works that are performed.

15. All of the writing and performance is for the Highest Good.

16. All of the writing and performance is done at a high level of consciousness.

17. I am a brilliant and prolific playwright and actress.

VI ~ Intentions for *Balm in Gilead*

1. I am brave.

2. I am inspired.

3. I radiate life.

4. We create an outstanding night of theater.

5. Billie's Intention: I create a safe, loving refuge for these characters . . . to warm their bodies/minds/spirits . . . to give comfort . . . to give love . . . to forget about myself . . . my life . . . and the past.

VII ~ Aliens to Dinner, by Duanita Gaye

In 1995 William "Pila" Chile's book, *The Secrets and Mysteries of Hawaii*, was published. In it he describes the paranormal experiences people have had on the Big Island of Hawaii and shares his 1970s prediction that "by the turn of the century they (aliens) would come to dinner" (p. 44). Well, it is now the 21st century, and I'm about to tell my friend to ask his alien friends to dinner with us.

About one week ago, my friend told me that he awoke to discover a beautiful woman sitting at the end of his bed. "I want to meet you," she said. "Where?" he asked. She named a large hotel and asked to meet him in the lobby.

Curious, my friend got dressed and drove to the hotel. He was surprised to see a doorman still working at that hour. When he entered the lobby he saw her again. She was around 75 years old with immaculate hair, face, and nails . . . impeccably dressed. Great legs. My friend describes her as the most beautiful 75-year-old woman he has ever met in his life. With her was an oriental looking man who was extremely physically fit.

They stood as my friend approached them. "We are very glad you came," the woman said extending her hand. My friend laughed when he related this first meeting to me. He told me that he wanted to shake both their hands just to feel if they were real. They were. My friend is a very scientific man, extremely skeptical of "visions" and anything else "illogical." He still thought he might be dreaming. They invited him up to their room to talk. They talked about scientific things and had information, which, according to my friend who is well educated technically, was far beyond what any human on earth has.

It was this "unworldly," profoundly deep level of information, which they were sharing with him, that made him wonder about whether or not they truly were human—that, and the nature of their eyes.

As my friend was leaving and shaking their hands in farewell, the woman said, "be sure to contact your friend," and she named me.

My friend was shocked. He had not mentioned me to them. He wondered how they knew about me. We had just had a major disagreement that had put a serious rift in our relationship. Why would these beings ask him to contact me?

My friend had been introduced to the whole pool of information about intentionality and quantum physics six months earlier through contact with me. Immediately upon beginning his intense study of this information, his dream life had changed significantly. He had begun having very "real" lucid dreams. He began experiencing a synchronistic, "miraculous" flow to his life.

At that point in time, we had ended our friendship. Suffice it to say that there were many reasons for this choice; however, the most significant reason for me was a choice to follow a dream I had when we were in the midst of our profound state of miscommunication.

In the dream, I was on a very small ferry with my friend and I knew beyond a doubt that I needed to jump ship. I leapt overboard and then realized that I had started up my friend's car just before I had jumped and that I had put it in drive. When I jumped ship I had done it in such a hurry that I had failed to put his car in park. The car came over the side of the ferry and was beginning to sink. In the dream I see I am in the wake of the ferry. I wake up.

As I awoke, I realized that in the dream, simultaneously, I had been a woman on shore watching all this happen. This woman had been wise. As this woman, I had realized before I went on the ferry that I was becoming what others wanted me to be. I had known that to go on the ferry was not what I really wanted. I would only be doing it to please others, my friend in particular. I knew that this would be wrong. As this woman, I made the choice in the dream to never get on that ferry. Even though my bags were packed and I was ready to go, I chose to turn around.

Upon waking, I was greatly disturbed by this dream. The miscommunication between my friend and I had been particularly intense. I had actively been praying to, and communicating with, my romance angels, my guides, and my spirits, asking for a sign, an image that would help guide me in my decision-making about this relationship. Needless to say, receiving an image of "jumping ship" brought to me profound feelings of loss and grief . . . yet the further my friend and I went down the rabbit hole of miscommunication, the more that I realized wisdom in the dream and in the choice of "jumping ship" in the relationship.

I come from a long line of women on my mother's side that have the gift of prophetic vision through dreams. I grew up knowing and trusting the wisdom of dreams. I grew up knowing the importance of being in relationship with dreams and acting upon them when and if necessary.

My formal study of my dreams and the dreams of my clients began in my early 20s and only served to reinforce and emphasize the learning of my youth.

So, after this dream, and after carefully considering the state of communication with my friend, I decided to follow my dream and "jump ship." I ended the relationship.

I was left alone, in profound grief, very much missing my friend yet with a deep knowing about the "rightness" of my choice. I have followed my dreams literally many times in the past and I have discovered that if I can just keep my faith and trust the dream and the process, even if the action seems strange, weird, or incredibly hard at the time, the reasons for the action and the wisdom of it are usually revealed in time.

In my formal training with dreams, I have learned a technique first written about by Carl Jung called "Active Imagination." It entails taking one's dream image and relating to it imaginally. In doing this, one acknowledges the independence and "life" of the images. One relates to it "as if" it is alive and "real." This engages a creative process that amplifies the original image, often providing profound insights. As Carl Jung puts it: "I watched the image . . . and then the image moved."

As "right" as the action in the dream seemed, I was greatly disturbed by one part in particular; the fact that because of me, my friend's car had idled off of the ferry and was sinking. I knew that this car was my friend's "baby." I knew how much it meant to him. I knew that the parallel grief for my friend caused by the loss of our relationship (no matter how bad the miscommunication had got) would be even greater than the loss of his car. I felt responsible for the unnecessary loss and grief. If only I had stayed out of my "pleasing" pattern altogether, or at the very least, realized what I was doing before I had got on to the ferry to make the journey with my friend . . . like the "other" wise part of me in the dream. If only I had stayed strong in my truth of what I wanted in a relationship. I could clearly see how a different choice could have prevented needless pain and suffering. I did recognize my pattern. I did it fairly early at the very beginning of that particular ferry journey. However, I also started the engine . . . and with that had caused damage. My friend's car had idled off the ferry and was sinking. I could clearly see the parallel of the relationship to the dream. If I had only never gotten on that ferry with my friend.

I entered the dream again in a state of active imagination:

> *I was in the water. The danger to me had passed as the ferry had moved off in the distance along with the wake which I had been concerned, at one point, would pull me under. In front of me was the sinking car. My friend had jumped in the water after me; however, several people were now pulling him back onto the ferry dock. The focus of the people onshore was the sinking classic car. It was like I was invisible.*
>
> *I swam to the other side of the shore and there was an old woman there who helped me into her house. She wrapped me up, placed me by the fire and brought me tea. She opened the curtains so that I could see across the bay to the ferry dock.*
>
> *I watched as they rescued the car. There had been a crane working on the ferry dock. It had simply turned and picked up the car and returned it to land before it had even begun to sink. It would be fine. I was so relieved I began to cry . . . and cry and cry and cry. Fortunately, the damage had been minimized. If this could only be true for the damage caused to my friend and my heart as a result of the ending of that journey in the relationship.*

My first contact with my friend happened about a week and a half after our relationship had "ended." I did not know if I should meet with him again. I was scared. I was asking for guidance—signs—daily with no results. I decided to meet with him rather than discuss what had happened either by telephone or email. I wanted to minimize the chances for miscommunication to happen.

As I drove to his house I played my tape by Doreen Virtue (2005), *The Romance Angels.* I had just started working actively with these angels when he and I first "connected." Each time I put the tape in I heard the angels' voices reminding me to "stay open to all possibilities." Even though

I thought the relationship was over, I set my conscious intention to be open.

He greeted me at the door with a long hug. "I am so happy you're here." I felt his body shaking. I heard a voice in my head say, "He is so vulnerable," a voice that repeated itself several times throughout our brief contact . . . particularly when he described his meeting with these two beings. As he stated so clearly, "Do you have any idea the impact such an encounter has on someone like me? I am a man of science. I have lived years without anything like this happening to me. Why me? Why now?"

I asked him if he had asked them why him. He replied, "Yes I did. They answered that I was special or something like that . . . nothing that made a lot of sense." I laughed. "That makes total sense," I said. "You are perfect. I know that you probably would have much preferred them to say something more 'scientific,' like—"Well actually your frontal lobe is firing at a frequency at which we vibrate making communication easily . . . blahblahblahblahblah." I stopped because I saw that my friend did not share my sense of humor. He really did not understand why the contact would be with him—a "nonbeliever" in such events. Yet I could easily see him as a perfect human through which to relay information that could alter the course of human history. He is incredibly intelligent, takes beautiful care of his physical body (no drinking or smoking; good diet), and has an intense curiosity.

Why now? Well, before I left I gave him a copy of Greg Braden's (2005) book tape, *Beyond Point Zero*, so that my friend might get a quick scientific overview of the crossroads in time at which we have arrived at this point in history.

We arranged to meet the following evening to attend the movie "*What the Bleep Do We Know!?*" (2004). It was a movie that another friend kept reminding me to see. Now that we had "connected" again, and after hearing of his "encounter," I asked him to come with me.

After the movie the next night, my friend informed me that the information he had been given during that initial encounter with the man and woman had been checked in two separate experiments and had been verified as being true. He was amazed. I had never doubted that this would be so.

I strongly encouraged him to develop his relationship with these beings. "Just tell them you want to meet again. They don't need a telephone or a phone. She demonstrated that in the first contact with you. You can just do the same. Say you want to meet with them again. Prepare a list of questions. And next time call me!" I joked, but only half-joked, since it has been one of my imaginings that someday I would be contacting such beings.

My interest and imaginings about contacting and being in relationship with other beings is a long story beginning with a dream I had in the early 1980s, when I was in my early twenties. In the dream: *I am in a classroom. A wise man at the front of the classroom points to a map on the wall. The map is clearly of the Big Island of Hawaii. On it is a red triangle. The man looks at me—points to the inside of the triangle and asks me, "Are you willing to enter evil?"*

At the time I took the dream to my wise friend. We were working intensely in the trenches at the beginning of the era of disclosures of incest and we had both witnessed the face of evil many times in our work. Her response to the dream was to ask, "Well, are you? Are you willing to enter evil?"

I remember being taken aback by her question. Part of me wanted to say "no," because I had seen enough to know how terrifying pure evil was. Another part of me responded, "Yes, I guess so. If there was someone in trouble or if there was a good reason. Yes. I think I would be willing. I wouldn't want to . . . I would prefer not to . . . but I would be willing if there was a good reason."

I have lived with this question for 20 years now. This is a way of being that I learned from my friend who works with dreams. When I have a dream and a good question to which I have no answer, I simply live with it and remain alert for any synchronicity connected to it.

It was in my late 30s, just before the turn of the century that the next connection to my dream and my question revealed itself.

I was going through the painful part of a divorce, my worldview totally and utterly shattered. I was in definite need of a vision quest. What was life about? Why was I here?

My daughter and I went to a mother-daughter spiritual retreat at Camp Quomais in White Rock, BC. Later I was to find out that "quomais" is a First Nations word for "vision." As I walked the stone labyrinth at the camp daily and looked out into the breath-taking vista, I prayed daily for a dream, a sign—something, anything—to help me know my purpose, my reason for being. What was the true meaning of life . . . because it certainly had not been about the illusion I had been living in my marriage.

One night I woke up with the following dream: "*I am in Hawaii and my friend Gwen introduces me to somebody.*"

I just laughed. I had no money or intention to go to Hawaii. Though it was a wonderful dream, I could not see how it was connected to the big questions I was asking at this point in my life. It did not "feel" like a vision for a purposeful vision quest. I had always imagined that when I did a vision quest the images would be earth shattering.

Five months later I understood the significance of the vision at a deeper level. My old roommate from my college days at University of Hawaii called. She was hosting a reunion in the spring and invited me. I really wanted to go. I remembered my vision and I knew that it was important for me to go. I was being called. The financial reality, however, was that I was newly separated with all the financial insecurity that can come from these new situations.

I remained open to the possibility, however, mainly because I had a sense that this trip was definitely connected with my vision and my life's purpose and direction. I had been working with Julia Cameron's (1992) book, *The Artist's Way: A Spiritual Path to Creativity*, for years and had seen miracles happen for my clients and me just simply by remaining open to the possibilities. Instead of saying "I can't do it," I had learned to say "How can I go to this reunion?" I wrote in my morning pages to the Universe that I could go if I had my credit cards paid off and I could pay cash for the trip.

Lo and behold I got a call. There was end-of-the-fiscal-year money that had to be spent before the end of March. I was asked if I would be willing to do some extra contract work on special contracts with my clients. Suddenly I had enough money to pay off all my credit cards and pay cash for the trip for my daughter and myself.

The Universe had responded and in April of 2001, about six months after my vision quest dream, I found myself at my friend Gwen's in Honolulu telling her of my vision and that she was to introduce me to someone. As it turned out that "someone" was William "Pila" Chiles. She introduced me to him by giving me his book, *The Secrets and Mysteries of Hawaii* (1995). When I read his book, he directly referred to the red triangle of my dream from the early '80s. I have since also learned of the phenomena of Poincare Maps through Hank Wesselman's book, *Visionseeker* (2001), in which he documents his visions, which began while living on a farm on the Big Island.

Pila's work (1995) specifically addressed UFO and paranormal activity, which is commonplace directly in line with the region identified to me as the red triangle on the Big Island in my 1980 dream. Pila also writes about the fact that the Big Island is actually one of the portals in this Universe where the veils between the worlds are very thin.

In my dream the man indicates that the area in which I would enter, if I were willing to enter evil, is this area on the Big Island. Ever since then, I have intuitively felt that someday I will have work to do on the Big Island and that this work will involve these UFOs.

I wrote Pila after arriving back in Canada, telling him of my intuition that I needed to do work on the Big Island. He wrote back and told me that he hoped I would connect to my work there as easily as "one plans a Sunday picnic."

Ever since 2001, I have been wondering when I would be called back to do the work. And what kind of work is it? My intuition tells me that I will be involved in the struggle between good and evil at a very different level than this reality. My intuition also tells me that I need to keep preparing myself for this journey. My biggest task right now is to learn how to completely transform my angry and fearful energy. I have come to know these as my character flaws. They are two areas that would be critical to transform into light before dealing with any evil forces.

Wesselman (2001) documents the plight of his friend Naiona who is a Hawaiian shaman living 5,000 years in the future. One small slip into anger at his nemesis caused Naiona's spirit guardian, Leopard Man, to move into protection mode. The nemesis was found killed by a leopard. Naiona was sent to a spiritual retreat to atone for his transgression. There is no room for the slightest bit of anger or fear when dealing with evil. When I get to the point of light in myself . . . then I will be ready.

How does this tie into my friend's "visitors"? Well, this is the closest I have ever gotten to contact with beings from other dimensions. This is the first time word has come to me that beings from other dimensions want me aware of their existence and want me to be in contact with someone that they are helping. Why? Why me? What is my role to be? Can they help me too?

The night my friend and I attended the movie and I encouraged him to develop a relationship with the unusual visitors; they visited him at his home. This time he called me, just as I had instructed him to, but I had turned my cell phone ringer off. Interestingly, though, I had woken up that night at around the same time of his call. When I awoke, I imagined that I got a call in the middle of the night to go out and visit with these beings. I asked myself, "Would you really want to go out?" I answered myself, "No. I would much rather be where I am with my daughter. Let them come to me."

As it turns out, on the second visit with my friend, the "visitors" gave him specific instructions for me. I was to see the movie *What the Bleep Do We Know!?* three times . . . once alone, then with a friend, and then alone. I was to take copious notes. Then I was to tell my friend all about it.

At first when I learned of the instructions I thought, "Yeah right! I am to do all this in three days (because the movie was being moved) while teaching every night, maintaining a full practice, single-parenting, and moving my studio?" Then I decided, "What do I have to lose?" I can no longer use "I have no time" as an excuse. If it was meant to be it will happen. I will simply ask "How can this become possible?"

When my friend told me of the first encounter and then the instructions given for me in the second encounter he kept saying that he hoped I believed him. I had only one small moment of questioning his honesty at the very first telling. I wondered if he was making this all up just to get me back. But I quickly dispelled the distrustful thought, because I could see his distress. He was afraid he was going crazy. I was the only one he could talk to at the time about the event (I have encouraged him to find a guide). I have had enough "strange and weird" experiences to know how awful it can feel when realities begin to blur. What he needed was a friend—someone to listen to him and support him and participate with him in whatever the "bleep" was going on!

Besides, to me it really does not matter. The image and the "visitors" were real to him. That is all that really matters. One day I may be included in that reality in order that I may participate more fully. Until then, I will do as I am instructed. After all, the way I look at it, what the bleep do I have to lose?

In the movie *What the Bleep Do We Know!?* I was most attracted to Dr. Joe Dispenza, because he talked about a practical way—a daily practice he does of actively co-creating reality. He asks for signs in which he is left with no doubt that he is an active co-creator with reality. I have begun to practice this daily since then, because I am very interested in the direct application of quantum physics to our realities. There is no time to "prove" the information presented. It is through living this information and experimenting with it that we will discover the truth.

I now realize that in working with my "jumping ship" dream, I consciously chose another reality. During this dream I was aware of being conscious in two characters simultaneously—the "me" that jumped ship and the "me" that recognized the old pattern and refused to go on the ferry in the first place.

In ending the relationship as it was in that dimension of reality I lived out the "me" that jumped ship. In that reality I also consciously connected to the "me" that refused to go on in the first place . . . the "me" who never got onto that ferry and had never started up my friend's car. I worked with active imagination to imagine what would have happened if I had been her. I wonder sometimes if I am living this possibility right now? What if I switched realities and have moved into a new experience—one in which I no longer get trapped in my addiction to please others?

When I met with my friend, the first time after we had "ended" the relationship, he also casually told me that the starter on his car had broken and was getting fixed. I find this fascinating. My friend had no idea of my dream . . . of my concern over "starting his engine." Yet here he was, telling me that in this reality his car would not start. Could this "starter problem" be another sign of the switch of realities to a new reality where my addiction to pleasing others is one that I can no longer even start?

So, therefore, I live in peace with all beings. I tell my friend to invite his "visitors" to dinner with us. I shift my consciousness easily. I can easily imagine this happening and thus . . . It becomes a possibility.

VIII ~ "Trusting Horse Sense," by Duanita Gaye

It was an unhealthy relationship pattern that compelled me to call a medical intuitive for help. I had gone around in a cycle of love, distrust, anger, fighting, sadness, doubt, forgiveness, love at least three times in the one year since I was in this new relationship. The last cycle had left me physically ill, having no energy, and bedridden for three days . . . a state that is extremely unusual for me.

Desperate for some help, I called. A distance reading of my chakras by the medical intuitive found me: well connected spiritually; intuitive to the point of clairvoyance; having a dark spot in my ability to communicate in this relationship; with my heart closed since I was protecting myself; and closed to the support of others.

It was one of the images she gave me, however, that I found the most helpful. She very clearly told me that the image she got of the relationship was that of control, not love. She said: I see you with a rope around your neck. *He feels he has to train you. He sees you as a young, untrained horse and is pulling you forcefully . . . yet he has no lesson to teach. And you, you have stars in your eyes. You have created an image of him as a creative person, yet it is your own creativity. He has caught you and now you cannot liberate yourself. He is pulling and you are unhappy.*

This image caught my attention for several reasons. First, when I was young, my family had called me a "kubilla," a Ukrainian word meaning "a wild female horse." My creative energy was explosive as a child and because I had no avenues of creative expression, it would often come out quite wild and exuberant. The second reason this image caught my attention is that I remembered this person actually saying once that I needed someone strong to "break" me, terminology that one would use when training a horse.

I then began doing the nine-day Novena, which was the recommended path of healing for me. Each day I cleansed myself. I cleansed my environment. I connected myself energetically with Source and I prayed for guidance on this issue. I was in a relationship pattern that was destructive and extremely unpleasant, yet which, despite all my knowledge and awareness and training, I found myself caught in.

On the third night of the Novena I had the following dream: *I am riding a horse through a store—like a fine china shop. Suddenly I realize how dangerous this is. I have been doing fine; however, there is such risk at doing damage. I realize this just as the shop ladies realize this. I ride the horse outside. The horse puts her head to the ground and the rope around her neck and I come off her. We slide down the horse's neck, over her head and off. I quickly move onto the horse again, in one swoop . . . securing the rope around her neck again smoothly and easily. The store woman says, "She'll just put you off again." I know she is right.*

In response to this dream, I used my active imagination where I simply never put the rope on the horse again or attempt to get on it and direct it. Instead, I trust the wisdom of the horse and I allow the horse to go free.

What I realized with these images was that it was never my partner who had me by a rope on my neck. All along it was me. Like a "bull in a china shop," I was taking my horse into inappropriate (indeed dangerous) places. I had put the rope around my own horse's neck and I could allow myself to be free any time I wanted.

I began to ponder my lack of trust of my "horse sense." "Horse sense" was a phrase I heard used often when I was a child. It referred to using one's common sense and/or using one's intuition.

Intuition and "horse sense" come from the realm of the illogical, the irrational, and the animal part of myself. Though I am strongly intuitive, I tend to doubt my horse sense. Like in the dream, I tend to discount the natural wisdom of my animal instincts and control and direct them with my will . . . with my intellect . . . with the logical and rational side of myself. Even if the horse knows that there is danger around and we really need to go outside, my intellect, my logical mind will override my instincts. I often disregard the messages and intentionally ride it into very dangerous situations.

I was never trained to trust my horse sense, my intuition . . . those niggling feelings . . . those strange thoughts that float through me. Usually when I have the feeling, I override it, doubt it, go against it, and end up regretting it later.

As a society we are under the influence of Newtonian thought where it is the concrete, practical, logical, and rational that is valued.

So . . . here the lesson is clear to me: If I trust my horse sense and release my need to control things logically, I am free. I am being asked to trust my "horse sense," trust my body, and trust my intuition. The irony is that not only am I being asked to trust my intuition, I am relying on the "horse sense" of another human being, the medical intuitive, a person I have never met in person. I do not even know what she looks like . . . yet I go to her to get advice about a really important decision in my life. And that is what she is relying on . . . her horse sense.

Trusting horse sense and relying on intuition requires me to surrender (my will in particular) and to have faith. I have learned to trust things that I can experience with my senses. If I saw concrete evidence that he was lying to me—if only someone told me something. I want some physical, logical reason to end the relationship. When I am asked to do it on the basis of intuition—I doubt myself . . . and as soon as I doubt my horse sense, I put the rope back on and attempt once again to wilfully steer my wiser self into dangerous ground . . . only to be gently removed time and time again.

An act of faith; an act of surrender. To honor images showing me the truth of the relationship. To trust a medical intuitive's images that he is closed to love; that he is not the partner for me; that we are on different levels of evolution. And even when the act of surrender and the leap of faith have been enacted, what then? One still needs to be able to move this decision into the real world . . . to take action.

This is where I had difficulty. Three months after the reading and the Novena . . . even though I knew her words, images, and her intuition gave strength, credence, and support to mine, I was still having trouble executing—bringing this through to reality—ending the relationship. I realized that this was mainly due to the fact that I would doubt myself. I would hold an intention, be clear and strong with it—then I would listen to his words, get confused, doubt myself, disregard the intuitive side of me, and I'd be in the cycle again.

Faith is a gift that I needed to give myself. I had to just trust that I was on the right track by ending the relationship and just doing it. I had to stop all doubt before it even surfaced. It was my intellect's way of sabotaging myself.

And what was I sabotaging? For the answer to this I went back to the medical intuitive's image of me with stars in my eyes. I have a pattern of projecting my own creativity in relationships with men whom I see as so creative, but who really are what Julia Cameron would call "blocked creatives." I pour my time, energy, and resources into the relationship and into supporting their creative development. I tell myself I do this for "them," that this is what a good partner does, etcetera, etcetera. Actually, I end up sabotaging myself and avoiding my own creative work. Instead of focusing on my creative work, I focus on all the bad things going on in the relationship.

Going to a medical intuitive helped me when I was desperate, in crisis. I already knew what she had to say—yet it helped to have my intuition confirmed by another human being. It was the synchronicity of images that helped to give me faith in our images.

I think that the recent appearance of "medical intuitives" is an indication that "horse sense" is becoming more and more acceptable as a legitimate way of knowing by the general population. We can go to others who are learning to tune in and trust this part of them, access this realm of information that is there for all of us. Ultimately, however, we are still faced with a decision of whether we have faith in this person and the purity of their connection. Can we surrender to the information we are given? Can we then execute on the information?

Ultimately, we still have to rely on our own horse sense, our own feeling of whether or not we can trust the information that is coming through irrational/illogical channels.

So, here is the end to my story.

Before the final meeting with this person, I wrote a friend seeking her guidance. My words reveal where I was at:

When I stay with the images and my intuition and even my experience, I know that I need to end this relationship to the point of no contact. When I hear his voice and I hear him talk about the grief it would cause him to lose me, I lose heart. It isn't that I question my decision; it is that I feel sorry for him. I no longer wish to cause such pain for another human being. I am scared to say the words, "Goodbye. I must leave you now. No contact please." Maybe I am even afraid of my own grief.

Once again, as in the past, my grief is over the disappearance of a dream, an illusion—who I think the person is rather than who they truly are. I have this habit of seeing the very best in people and being blinded to and blindsided by their dark sides.

I know I must do this . . . and I know I will be fine . . . and I know he will be fine. Yet I feel so cold and cruel. I wonder: Am I giving this enough chances? Am I giving him a chance? Am I giving us a chance?

Even as I write this I know that there is no chance. The issues are way too severe.

All I can do now is hold the intention and ask for the Great Creator's help to end this relationship in the best and easiest way for everyone . . . for the Highest Good of All.

He was unusually late to pick me up for our last meeting. I decided to sit on some comfy chairs in the corner coffee shop while I waited. I was sitting there praying to the Universe for help: *I know what I must do based on intuition, yet I would really like some physical signs that I must end the relationship with him, that what I am doing is right. I would like something that I can see with my eyes and hear with my ears.*

At that moment a young man came up to me and asked if he could sit with me. He introduced himself as Peter Sammarco and gave me an invitation to hear his lecture on his new book *The Five Pillars of Relationships* (2005). He said that he had been watching me and something just told him that he was to come over and talk with me. He was nervous and talking incessantly. This gave me a moment to realize that he was my angel and he had the message that I needed to hear. So I said, "Actually, I am now in a relationship where there are major problems with trust."

He cut me off with a very clear and blunt response. "The problem isn't in the relationship. The "problem" is with you. You don't trust yourself. That is why you are creating relationships where there is no trust. Once you start trusting yourself you will attract relationships where this isn't an issue."

There it was again. The same message. The message in my dream . . . the message that the medical intuitive gave me. I was still having trouble trusting myself, my horse sense, and my intuition.

Then I asked him, "Well, is there any way to end a relationship and have no pain for anyone involved?" I was still concerned with hurting the person in the relationship. Peter responded, "A loss is always a loss . . . and one has to remember that though you end the relationship, it still remains always a part of both of you."

Then he said something that seemed to shock even him. "You also need to remember that there are other men out there right now who can benefit from your love. You need to trust yourself and move on." At that moment my friend drove up in the car and it was time for me to leave.

As I sat in the final meeting with the man I needed to leave, Peter's final words rang in my ears. It was time for me to move on. There was someone else out there that needed my love.

Believe it or not, despite all the signs—the dreams, intuition, angels— as I sat there, I still needed something more. As my friend droned on and on, I was praying: *Please, please let me see or hear something. Help me to know for sure that my decision to end this relationship and have no more contact is the right one.*

My prayer to hear something to help me move on was soon answered. During the conversation he unwittingly revealed that he had been lying in a very serious manner to me during the course of the relationship. I did nothing to give away the fact that I had discovered him in his lie. It was a huge lie. I sat, grateful that I now knew this was the case for sure—shocked that another human could sit and lie so calmly face to face with someone that they claimed to love.

Despite this, I still thought that I should give him a final chance to come clean with the truth.

"Okay, I have heard everything you had to say. Is there anything else you wish to tell me at this time?" I asked.

"No," he replied.

I decided to give him one more last chance.

"Are you sure that you have nothing more to tell me?" Inside I think I was truly hoping that he would admit his lie. I think I was hoping this so that I would still be able to have faith in the honesty of people.

Then it happened. My prayer was answered to see something to help me in my desire to know for sure.

I sat and watched as his eyes rolled back and fluttered for what seemed like an eternity. I am a trained clinical therapist who has worked with severely wounded people and I had seen this behavior before. It was the prolonged shifting of the eyes that happens with people who have severe dissociative disorders.

I sat and watched in utter shock, amazement, and even disbelief. I knew I had to watch. I had to see. I had to remember. I had asked to see a sign with my own eyes, a sign that would definitely help me move forward with my final decision. This was clearly it.

He came out of the episode, looked me in the eye, and replied to my question: "Nothing at the present time."

His voice was chilling. The choice of words was unusual for him. I did not recognize his eyes. They were suddenly dull and dead . . . soulless. I did not see him in them. In fact, I would say that I saw no spark of life in them. A voice in me wondered who was actually sitting across from me. In the moment, I felt an alien presence. I wondered if an alien spirit had possessed my friend. I sensed that the intention behind the spirit was murderous. I was not afraid; rather, I felt concern for my friend. It is a long story that I will not go into right now; however, my friend had told me of contact that he had had with two alien entities that had begun three months after we had connected. At the time he had been very shocked and scared to death that he was going crazy. He had told me bits and pieces of his contacts with these two entities throughout our relationship. I had questioned the motives of these beings and he had slowly stopped giving me detailed information about his encounters with them.

It was as though an unspoken conversation was going on between me and this presence that had taken over in the meeting. The presence knew that I had recognized the change in my friend. It was almost like it challenged me to say anything consciously about the shift. I sensed that the best response to the change that I had witnessed was to end the conversation by saying, "OK then."

When we were walking out of the restaurant, my friend walked ahead of me. If I had stopped, he would not have noticed. This behavior was also very unlike my friend, so much so that I noted it. Even if my friend had been angry with me, he would never have been so disconnected. We walked to the car in silence. The relationship was over.

I wonder sometimes if my horse sense, my intuition, and feelings during that last meeting with my friend are indeed true. Sometimes I want to question them; I want to doubt myself. However, I know one thing for sure, the memory of his eyes shifting was very real. It is burned in my memory. It is what I keep going back to, to give me the strength to stay with my resolve.

Sometimes I wonder if my friend needs help. Then I remember; the relationship is over. No contact.

References

Cameron, J. (2002). *The artist's way*. New York: Penguin Putnam.

Cerepnalkoski, L. (2005). Medical Intuitive. Consultation, June 2005. 310-772-8270

Sammarco, P. (2005). *The five pillars of relationships: Be the creator of your own world*. Victoria: Tafford Publishing.

IX ~ "Signs," by Duanita Gaye

In the "Create Your Day" activity as outlined by Dr. Joe Dispenza (2004), the final part of the morning invocation is a request that there be a "sign" given that the intention has been received by the quantum field and is being addressed. There is a special request that the sign be of the kind that leaves no doubt that it comes from Source.

What confused me most as I reviewed my daily writings was that though I requested such signs, and though these signs are crucial to me in helping to fuel my faith, conviction, and commitment, I rarely wrote down the signs I was receiving throughout the immersion process. This omission from my daily writings puzzled me because I know how important signs are for me and I have seen how important they are to others doing this work. They can make the difference between someone doing the work or not. So why was I negligent in recording the signs?

What Are Signs?

Doreen Virtue (2005) talks about signs as blessings and answers from Heaven. For her, signs are:

Messages that you see or hear repetitively . . . notice anything that you see or hear three or more times. For instance, if several people recommend the same book, movie, or class to you that's a sign. Observe unusual occurrences, such as angel-shaped clouds or clusters of butterflies. Pay attention to items with special significance, such as a loved one's favorite song playing on the radio, or a flower that you associate with a particular person or event. (p. 77)

I love the way Dr. Wayne Dyer (2006) speaks of signs as "the language of spirit" and how he puts the emphasis on signs being the way that our Spiritual Source is getting in touch with us.

What both Dyer and Virtue stress is never to dismiss signs as "coincidence" since communication patterns of Spirit may seem strange, weird, unusual, and/or illogical. Virtue (2005) reminds us of the old adage that "coincidences are when God remains anonymous" (p. 78).

But What Do They Mean?

On the very day I realized that (though I love getting signs and though they affirm my faith in what I am doing and though I had been asking for signs daily as part of my "Create My Day" practice) I had neglected to document the signs that were given to me in response to my requests, I was blessed with the appearance of three of my totem animals; the hummingbird, the wolf, and the bear.

It was a summer day and I had a rare chance of going to visit one of my friends in Brackendale, BC, to celebrate her birthday, which had passed the month before. I was highly conscious that ever since my realization in the morning that I was neglecting to write about signs and give them due attention, the Universe had been pouring on the delivery of signs, which seemed to indicate that I had hit on something.

For example, in the waiting room in my studio I have a deck of cards by Wayne Dyer, quotes from his book Inspiration: Your Ultimate Calling (2004). Before I began work that day I pulled a "Message of the Day," which told me to watch for synchronicities that day. I smiled, since even getting that card was synchronous to my intentions of how I would co-create the day. To me getting the card was a sign confirming that the Universe was responding and telling me, "Yes indeed. You are on the right path. Watch for the signs. Pay attention to the signs."

Just as I ended work, I got a phone call from a client whom I had seen earlier in the day. While she was with me I had laughingly given her a philosophy of life that I had learned from one of my students. It was the philosophy of Mary Kay, a woman who herself achieved great success in life and who helped many others achieve success. The philosophy is: God (or Spirit . . . or as I named it for this client . . . inner work) first, family second, and career third. I had laughed when I told this client the philosophy because I would usually never quote Mary Kay in my practice . . . yet for this client it seemed to fit.

Her voice mail message was to tell me that after seeing me she had met up with a friend who gave her a belated birthday present: some Mary Kay products. This client said that she had never before received or bought Mary Kay products and that the synchronicity of this occurrence on the very day that I so hesitantly told her Mary Kay's philosophy made her feel that this was a sign for her to follow that philosophy in her own life. She also noted in the message: "I know signs are important to you and I just thought you would like to know."

I smiled. To me her call was a sign. That this happened on the very day I was affirming the importance of signs and addressing my neglect in writing them down was affirmation of the importance of this area to my research.

Just as I receive a very deep resonating affirmation from signs that give me faith and courage and even bolster my energy and motivation to pursue particular paths, so too do my clients. Signs may seem a strange thing for a therapist to be teaching clients, yet I have found over the years that signs can provide confidence, faith, and courage for clients in powerful ways to which I only wish I had immediate access as a therapist. I have seen signs lift people, reconnect people to a greater understanding of the meaning of life and their place in it. I have seen depressed and hopeless people become animated and inspired overnight because of a sign. I have seen people gain the perseverance and commitment necessary to do inner work when given a sign.

My client's story also carried with it another message. As well as affirming the importance of people knowing about signs, it also affirmed that my appreciation and understanding of signs was important in my practice. My client paid attention to the sign she was given, was aware of it, and even noticed it partly because she knew that signs are important to me.

Most times, as in the case of this woman, I am unaware of when I am teaching about signs. I never formally went through any information with this woman dealing with signs. So how did she know signs are important to me?

I was talking to one of my friends the other day, guiding him through a rough spot in his life, when suddenly he said, "I love how you do that." "Do what?" I asked. "You talk about signs, you always refer to signs. You did that with your daughter the other day and I just loved it." I realized that I had been unaware of how often I refer to signs with people, and also unaware of how, for most people, this may not be a consideration within their usual realm of conversation. I realized that I pretty much constantly look for, refer to, and want to understand signs. I do live what I talk about with signs, and people are learning just by watching who I am, what I say and do, and how I live my life—often while I am unaware that it is happening.

These stories, of my client's and my friend's experience and perception of me with regard to signs leaves me with a deep knowing that, in some ways, in the arena of signs, I am being the change I want to see in the world. To me, knowledge, awareness, and understanding of signs, of the language of Spirit, is a crucial tool to be able to live in a paradigm that honors the illogical, the irrational, the Creative Spirit that moves through everything and connects us all as one. I am living this reality and learning daily how to live it to an even deeper degree. Through living this reality I am impacting and fostering change with ripples that I sometimes see and hear about from people I know . . . and many unseen ripples that I can only imagine at this point. Signs are, and have been, an important part of my daily reality for quite a time.

After I left work, the miracles only continued. I met my friend and we went for a walk and talk in the area of Brackendale, BC, where the bald eagles come home to nest every year. While we were there, we were visited by my first totem animal, the wolf.

As we sat on the bench talking, a dog that was obviously part wolf approached us. The next day when we spoke of this profound experience in an attempt to understand the message of it, we both thought the dog was a male, mostly because it was huge with long wolf legs and a lean wolf body. It was also obviously an old character and was very skittish.

My friend had watched it approach us coming from the road and had wondered if it was with a woman walking another dog off in the distance. As we talked, only initially half-aware of its presence, it circled us, close to the back of the bench and around the front, really working hard to get our attention, yet too skittish to approach directly.

We stopped talking and finally looked at him, paying more attention to what was going on. He stopped and began staring at us. As I held eye contact with him, I had an image from my Wolf Dream (2000), in which a female wolf broke from a pack of wolves, ran straight up to me and locked a gaze with me about a foot from my face. The image had been extremely powerful at that time in my life, because I had been in the process of getting divorced and this image (and my subsequent exploration into the habits and nature of the wolf) became my guide with regard to how to live as a "lone wolf," powerful and strong in my dedication to my new single-parent family reality.

When this image flashed through my head, I became acutely aware that I needed to pay attention, that this was another sign, that the Universe had sent me one of my totem animals. At first, part of me was tempted to simply say "thank you" and chalk it up to just another affirmation response from the Universe. But the dog/wolf could not be so easily dismissed.

After staring at us from a distance, he put his head down and began to initiate an approach that made me think that he might be thirsty (it was one of BC's unusually hot summer days). My friend told me later that her thought was that he might be hungry. Growing up in Pemberton, BC, with a dog and a horse as her closest childhood companions, she knew animals and the land in an intimate way. This knowledge made her immediately dismiss thirst as a reason for the dog/wolf's behavior, since she knew that even though he was an old dog, he would go down the fairly easy path to the river in front of us to drink if he were thirsty.

My friend then moved her shoes. The sound of them on the sidewalk startled the dog/wolf, making him jump and move in to circle behind us again. I had a brief moment of fear, which passed into an acute awareness of this dog/wolf. He now had our full attention. We knew he wanted to communicate something. We just were not clear as to what.

He then walked over to the end of the path where there was a huge iron, chain-link gate. He stood there and looked at us, and then up at the sign . . . us . . . and then up at the sign. At this point I was telling my friend that this animal was a sign and we were verbally attempting to figure out what he wanted.

My dog Nikki has a way of focusing his eyes on my food . . . then looking at me briefly, then focusing back on my food, then looking at me briefly, when he wants to draw my attention to the fact that he would like me to give him my food. This dog/wolf was doing the same thing. His focus was on the sign. I understood his communication so I looked at this huge sign that I had not really noticed before. I remembered that on that day my job was to pay attention to signs and I realized that this could easily include literal signs, so I read the sign: "NO TRESPASSING."

At the moment I also had a flash from my childhood of a show I used to watch called "Littlest Hobo." It was about a dog that wandered around the earth saving and helping people. In the show, the dog would often be telling the humans something like, "Follow me. Come quick." I remember the agony I felt as a child when I watched the humans in the show often being so slow to get the communication. As I watched this dog/wolf working so hard to communicate something to us, I briefly wondered if I would have the faith, understanding, and willingness to follow a dog's guidance. Would I be responsive enough to the communications from the animal world to be able to stop and change my behavior in order to listen?

As we watched and realized he wanted us to read the "No Trespassing" sign, I began talking to him out loud. "What? What? Okay. No trespassing. We got that." Then it appeared as though he wanted to go through. I wondered if he wanted us to follow him. I wondered how he could get through or how I could help him through.

Then he looked at us meaningfully and indicated a hole in the fence right beside the locked gate with a sign on it. We had not noticed this hole before. He gave one glance back at us and then slipped through the hole, which seemed almost like it had been made for him. He was gone quickly without a backward glance, leaving both of us extremely moved.

When we got back to my friend's house, we sat on her porch as the hummingbirds buzzed around us, and then we went to her neighbor's phenomenal garden. As my friend showed me around the garden with all its beauty, I noticed that I had a judgmental thought about the plywood cut-outs that the woman had placed in the garden.

Then as we delighted in yet another plant, we both stopped as a tiny black bear, most likely a yearling, made his way out of the bush behind the houses and began crossing the yard. I was floored at the sight, since I recognized him as yet another powerful sign. The bear had been another of my totem animals that came to me during my profound mystical initiation henna experience, in Egypt, with the Nubian women. The Universe had responded to my intention for that day with regard to signs by allowing me to experience three of my totem animals. I was moved.

We came off the neighbor's balcony. I thought we were going to go and ensure that my friend's dog was safe in the house next door. But instead of going home, my friend began to follow the bear. I followed her quietly, realizing that I was actually experiencing some fear and would have much preferred that we move to the safety of her home. The next day when I asked her about her actions, she told me that she always does this. If there is a bear in the neighborhood, she goes out, follows it, and watches out of curiosity and because she loves them. She enjoys watching them, seeing what they do, and she likes to remember them so that she knows them when they come by.

This revelation from her shocked me into an awareness of how far I was from ever thinking this way about bears. About coyotes, wolves, and other critters I had grown up with on the prairie in Canada, I might have been inclined to do this. But since moving to BC my only education about bears has been safety. I realized that I was also being educated to fear rather than to follow bears.

The next day my friend called me with the question, "What was the message of the dog/wolf sign?" We both knew it was an extra-ordinary experience. We both felt the awe, mystery, and urgency of the dog/wolf in ensuring that the message was communicated—that we saw it and we got it.

I told her that I did not know. As is so often the case, I may get signs, be aware enough to recognize them, recognize their importance, and yet fail to understand them.

When I had come home from my friend's, though I knew I was being told that, yes, it was important for me to write about signs, I found I couldn't write. I forced myself to jot down a list of the signs I had seen that day so that I could at least set the intention to write about that magical, mystical day.

The next morning I brought out the list, intending to write, and I found that I did not even complete my usual three pages of morning writing. I found myself staring into space during a major portion of my writing time, and leaving my writing unfinished, which is extremely rare for me to do.

My friend's call and question realigned me to my work. I realized I was not writing about my experiences because: they were so overwhelming that it was almost like a shock reaction; and sometimes when experiences so sacred happen, I wonder if it is wise to share them or if they lose their power somehow in the sharing. My initiation in Egypt experiences, for example, have been shared with very few people, though as time passed I found myself more willing to share. I didn't know what to write, because I had no idea what it all really meant. I got that it was Spirit speaking very clearly to me through humans, and objects, and animals—yet what exactly was the message?

Through the process of my friend and I unravelling and making sense of the dog/wolf experience and pondering and brainstorming around the question, "What is the message?," I realized many things about signs. First, like dreams, their messages are multilevel. As with any good story or myth, the individuals experiencing the sign will gain insight and understanding at precisely the level they need. I used to ask the question, "What is the message of the sign?" expecting a nice, neat, tight answer. I now realize that Spirit does not unusually communicate this way. Signs, like dreams, usually have many levels of messages. Therefore, this experience has prompted me to ask better questions like, "What are the messages inherent in the sign?," or, "What is being communicated?"

Dyer (2006) wrote that in his quest to understand the language of spirit, he immediately notes what he is thinking, talking about, or doing when a sign happens:

A few times in my life, I've had a bird sweep by my body, and on each of these occasions I've felt a deep sense of connection to God. Each time I've stopped and re-examined my thoughts at the precise instant of contact, and I was able to interpret that connection as a message to pay closer attention to my mission of writing. (p. 229)

When my friend contacted me to ask what I thought the sign of the dog/wolf meant, I applied this insight and so we asked the questions: "What were we talking about when this sign occurred? How is the sign a metaphor for the issue we were discussing? What is the message of the metaphor for us?"

At the moment that the dog/wolf appeared, my friend and I were deep in a discussion about my ethical dilemma. I was faced with choices about whether or not to keep corresponding online with a man that I just discovered was engaged. Years after I had met this man at a conference, his name had popped up on my computer screen in a very unusual place. I took this as a sign to contact him, so I emailed him saying that I was not sure why I was contacting him; however, his name had popped up and I thought it might be a message to contact him.

As it turns out, he had been thinking of me and had been searching through old contact information to find my email address. As it also turned out, he was engaged and unhappy about the engagement and questioning whether or not to get married. He explained that he really wanted to get married but that his fiancée wanted to remain engaged rather than moving through to marriage.

After he wrote me this, I had many synchronistic events happen in my life, which indicated that I needed to really look at my motives for continuing contact with this man. When I was truly honest with myself about what kind of relationship I wanted with this man, I realized that I had been fooling myself by saying that I just wanted a "friendship." I was actually very physically attracted to him. Even if it was a distance relationship through emails, I would want our relationship to be one where sexual energy was exchanged. In fact, I realized that, to some degree, this had already been happening.

As soon as I realized this, I wrote him an email telling him what I had discovered about myself and my intentions toward him. I suggested that if he truly wanted his engagement to work through to marriage, as he had said, then it was probably best for him to seal up all energy levels by ending relationships like the one with me. I guessed that his fiancée did not know about me and suggested that some of her hesitation to commit fully to him might be that she senses that there are connections that he has that she does not know about, connections that interfere, and rightly so, with her ability to trust him.

After I emailed this letter to him, my private practice became a superhighway where cases of people in relationships having close emotional connections with others online began popping up daily. One client even taught me the new buzzword for this relatively new phenomenon: "emotional affairs." The problem with emotional affairs is that they can drain the life force out of the primary relationship—that is, the relationship that has supposedly been sealed by a commitment between two people. Another problem is that often people do not recognize this as an "affair," since we seem to have a bias toward a definition of "affair" as penis-vaginal intercourse in our society and assume that only if this happens, then it is an affair that can cause damage.

This has been a question of mine for years. When does an "affair" start? When people kiss? When they touch genitals? When they masturbate to someone else's image? When they have thoughts of being with another person? Or is it only when the act of penis-vaginal intercourse occurs, as society would have us define an affair up to this point in history?

Our new understanding of energy and how it works and how it is exchanged between people brings up many new issues in relationships and many new ethical questions, which I have been wondering about and questioning people about for quite some time. Mostly because, over and over again, I see people having affairs, or getting involved with married people (or people who are in a committed relationship) and telling me "I don't know how it happened. I never would have seen myself with a married man." And yet, it happens and people find themselves there, and why?

The ethical dilemma I was facing in the situation in which I found myself was whether or not to cross the line and correspond with this engaged man and let him pour his heart out to me, a woman with far-from-pure intentions with regard to him, instead of talking about these issues with his fiancée. If I had allowed myself to hide my sexual feelings toward him, I could have just allowed myself to be carried unconsciously, ignore the fact that he had a fiancée, talk with him deeply (about his heart, his fears about commitment and marriage, his concerns about her)—all in the guise of helping a friend. I could have ignored the fact that his connection with me was being kept from his fiancée (not to mention ignoring the reasons why this was so), which is an act of lying by omission in a relationship, and which has implications about what he would be like in relationship with me. What are the chances that he is having other connections with women like me without telling me? What would make me think that this man would be faithful and loyal to me, even as a friend, if he would lie by omission to his fiancée and turn to others like me to share his heart?

I dug deeper into my motives, and at the time when the wolf sign appeared in my life, I was making a decision about whether or not to keep corresponding with this man, which would mean that I would be making a conscious decision to be an online emotional lover.

My friend and I discussed the metaphor of "no trespassing" when it comes to marriage and engagement. In our society, the ethical rule is that when someone is married or engaged they have committed themselves to another individual and that bond/commitment is meant to be respected by them as well as by others. It is an ethical rule similar to the fence to which the dog/wolf brought our attention, a fence that was protecting land from trespassers.

Our ethics are what form the "fence," so to speak, around our relationships. The rule is clear: No trespassing. Yet in that natural setting it becomes obvious that the fence and the sign are manmade. Our ethics and where the fence is put up are a result of our ideas and beliefs about relationships. In that natural setting with the dog/ wolf, it also became clear that though we put up signs and fences as barriers to protect these areas, there are ways around them. If we look, we can choose to go with our wild wolf instinctual parts and cross manmade ethical barriers—easily.

The action of the dog/wolf made me wonder if the message was for me to cross the line. I could come up with all kinds of really good rationalizations of why I could do that. But ultimately, I did not feel good about crossing into forbidden territory.

And then I thought about how maybe the lesson for me is that signs are different for different people. For others the message might be to cross the line. For me, the dog/wolf just wanted to ensure that I saw the no trespassing sign. Now it could have been any animal, but it was the animal that came to me in the past at a time where I needed to go it alone and learn how to be alone. And for me it was highly significant that the dog/ wolf never stopped when he went under that fence to signal us to follow him. He did not want me to follow him into the territory where the rules are broken. He wanted me to see the sign: "No Trespassing."

For me, at this point in my life, with the work I am doing to always be a person of integrity to the best of my ability, and to always choose Truth, the message is that indeed I have a choice to stop at the fence and simply see the hole or to go through despite the sign. And I can see that sometimes manmade rules need to be broken, and sometimes is it crucial to break them. With the situation that I was facing, my choice would be to respect the sign.

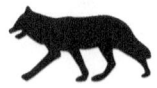

About The Author

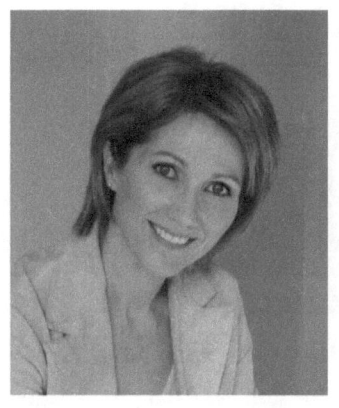

Duanita G. Eleniak, Ph.D., is a registered clinical social worker, registered art therapist, philosopher, writer, and educator. She loves to facilitate relationships with images in all their various forms: dreams, words, thoughts, beliefs, play, sand tray, and a variety of art media. She is always honored to midwife the changes that happen for people and groups when they establish deep connection and intimacy with their authentic selves as expressed through their images. Her current focus is on teaching and supporting people to shift emotions in order to facilitate an increase in their quality of life and an ability to sustain feelings of love, joy, and peace. On a larger scale, Dr. Duanita is committed to assisting the paradigm shift from the current dominant worldview, sometimes referred to as "scientific materialism," to a worldview that incorporates Spirit and has a deep respect for mystery. She lives with her daughter and woofies in North Vancouver, BC, Canada.

Other Books By The Author

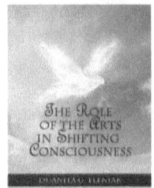

Role Of The Arts In Shifting Consciousness

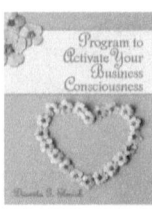

Program To Activate Your Business Consciousness

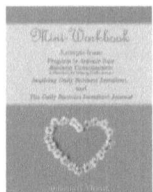

Mini Workbook For Program To Activate Your Business Consciousness

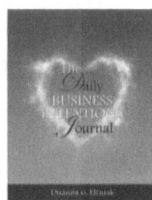

The Daily Business Intentions Journal

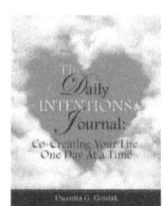

The Daily Intentions Journal

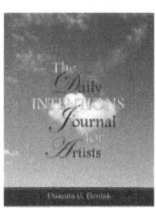

The Daily Intentions Journal For Artists

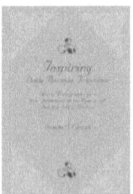

Inspiring Daily Business Intentions

Courses Available At http://www.mentoringstore.ca

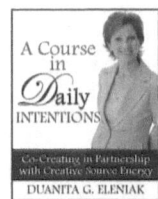

Daily Intentions

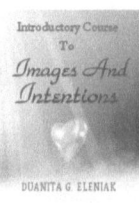

Images And Intentions

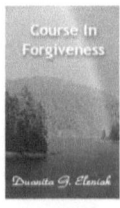

Course In Forgiveness

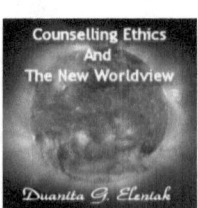

Counselling Ethics And The New Worldview

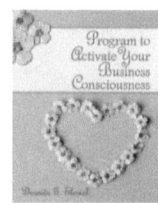 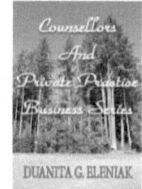 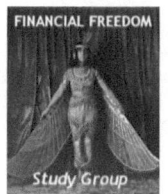

Program To Activate Your Business Consciousness   **Counsellors And Private Practice Business Series**   **Financial Freedom Study Group**

Course Available At The American Art Therapy Association Career Center at

http://arttherapy.trainingcampus.net/uas/modules/trees/windex.aspx

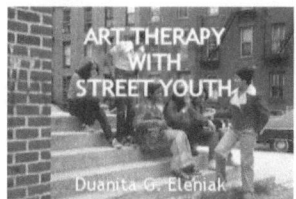

Art Therapy With Street Youth

Resources

For information on publications, workshops, and seminars by Dr. Duanita, or to place an order, please see:

Website: http://www.mentoringstore.ca

I hope that you enjoyed this journey and that it has somehow made a difference for you. I would love to hear from you. If you wish to share your experience reading this book, or for a copy of the student films referred to, please contact:

The Mentoring Store
#201-431 Mountain Highway
North Vancouver, British Columbia
Canada V7J 2L1
1-604-988-5689

Email: info@mentoringstore.ca

Select Bibliography

Arntz, W., Chasse, B., & Vincente, M. (Producers). (2004). *What the bleep do we know!?* [Movie]. California: Twentieth Century Fox Film Corporation.

Braden, G. (2005). *Beyond zero point* [Audio CD]. May 30, 2001.

Braden, G. (2004). *The God code.* Carlsbad, CA: Hay House.

Braden, G. (2002). *Isaiah effect: Decoding the lost science of prayer and prophecy.* Carlsbad, CA: Hay House.

Braden, G. (2001). *An ancient magical prayer: Insights from the Dead Sea scrolls.* Carlsbad, CA: Hay House.

Byrne, R. (2006). *The secret* [movie]. Australia: TS Production.

Cameron, J. (1992). *The artist's way: A spiritual path to higher creativity.* New York: Penguin Putnam.

Campbell, J. (1988). *Interview with Bill Moyers.* PBS Special.

Capra, F. (1975). *The Tao of physics.* New York: Bantam Books.

Castaneda, C. (1971). *A separate reality: Further conversations with Don Juan.* New York: Simon & Schuster.

Chasse, B. & Vincente, M. (2004). *What the bleep do we know!?* Available on DVD at www.whatthebleep.com

Chekhov, M. (1985). *Lessons for the professional actor*. New York: Performing Arts Journal Publications.

Chile, W. (1995). *The secrets and mysteries of Hawaii*. Deerfield Beach, FL: Health Communications.

Clements, J. (2000). *Organic inquiry: Theory*. Unpublished manuscript.

Clements, J. (2001). *Organic inquiry: Researching in partnership with spirit*. Unpublished manuscript.

Clements, J., Ettling, D., Jennett, D., & Shields, L. (1998). *Organic inquiry: If research were sacred*. Palo Alto, CA: Serpentine Press.

Combs, A. (2002). *The radiance of being: Understanding the grand integral vision: Living the integral life*. New York: Omega Books.

Curry, D. & Wells, S. (2003). *An organic inquiry primer for the novice researcher: The who, what, when, why, and how of a sacred approach to disciplined knowing*. Washington: Liminal Realities.

Diamond, J. (1979). *Behavioral kinesiology*. New York: Harper & Row.

Dispenza, J. (2005). *Rewiring your brain to a new reality* [CD from the 2005 Conference Series What the Bleep Do We Know!?], Santa Monica, CA: February 5, 2005.

Douglas, N., & Slinger, P. (2000). *Sexual secrets: The alchemy of ecstasy*. Rochester,VT: Destiny Books.

Dyer, W. (2006). *Inspiration: Your ultimate calling*. Carlsbad, CA: Hay House.

Dyer, W. (2001). *There is a spiritual solution to every problem*. Carlsbad, CA: Hay House.

Dyer, W. (2004). *The power of intention*. Carlsbad, CA: Hay House.

Emery, J. (1998). *Win the audition: Use the power of your mind to achieve acting success*. [Audiocassette]. U.S.A.: For Actors Only.

Emoto, M. (2004). *The hidden messages in water.* Carlsbad, CA: Hay House.

Ferrer, J. & Tarnas, R. (2001). *Revisioning transpersonal theory: A participatory vision of human spirituality.* Albany: State University of New York Press.

Ford, T. (2006, March). *Tom Ford's New Hollywood: The 2006 Portfolio.* Vanity Fair, 285-331.

Gandhi, M. (2006). *Quoteland.* Retrieved November 3, 2006, from http://www.quoteland.com/author.asp?auth

Gendlin, E. T. (1997). *Experiencing and the creation of meaning: A philosophical and psychological approach to the subjective* (Rev ed.). Evanston, IL: Northwestern University Press.

Goodheart, G. (1976). *Applied kinesiology* (12th ed.) Detroit, MI: Privately Published.

Grof, S., & Bennet, H. (1993). *The holotropic mind: The three levels of human consciousness and how they shape our lives.* New York: HarperCollins.

Hagelin, J. (2004). *Manual for a perfect government.* Carlsbad, CA: Hay House.

Hart, T., Nelson, P., & Puhakka, K. (2000). *Transpersonal knowing: Exploring the horizon of consciousness.* Albany: State University of New York Press.

Hawkins, D. R. (2005). *Truth vs. falsehood.* Toronto, Canada: Axial.

Hawkins, D. R. (2004). *The impact of spontaneous spiritual experiences in the life of "ordinary" persons.* Watkins Review, 7.

Hawkins, D. R. (2002). *Power versus force: An anatomy of consciousness.* (Rev. ed.). Carlsbad, CA; Brighton-le-Sands, Australia: Hay House.

Hawkins, D. R. (2001). *The eye of the I: From which nothing is hidden.* Sedona, AZ: Veritas.

Hawkins, D. R. (2000). *Consciousness and a course in miracles* [Videocassette]. Sedona, AZ: Veritas.

Hawkins, D. R. (1995). *Quantitative and qualitative analysis and calibration of the levels of human consciousness.* Ann Arbor, MI: VMI, Bell and Howell Col.; republished 1999 by Veritas, Sedona, AZ.

Hawkins, D. R. (1995). *Power versus force; Consciousness and addiction; Advanced states of consciousness: The realization of the presence of God; Consciousness: How to tell the truth about anything; Undoing the barriers to spiritual progress* [Videocassettes]. Sedona, AZ: Veritas.

Hawkins, D. R. (1987). *Drug addiction and alcoholism: A map of consciousness; Cancer (audio only); AIDS; and Death and dying.* [Sedona lecture series. Audio/videocassettes]. Sedona, AZ: Veritas.

Hawkins, D. R. (1986). *Stress; Health; Spiritual first aid; Sexuality; The aging process; Handling major crisis; Worry, fear and anxiety; Pain and suffering; Losing weight; Depression; Illness and self-healing; and Alcoholism* [Office Series. Audio/videocassettes]. Sedona, AZ: Veritas.

Hawkins, D. R. (1985). *Consciousness and addiction. In S. Burton and L. Kiley, Beyond addictions, beyond boundaries.* San Mateo, CA: Brookridge Institute.

Hay, L. (1998). *Self-esteem affirmations: Subliminal mastery series.* Carlsbad, CA: Hay House.

Hay, L. (1997). *Empowering women: Every woman's guide to successful living.* Carlsbad, CA: Hay House.

Hay, L. (1995). *Life! Reflections on your journey.* Carlsbad, CA: Hay House.

Hay, L. (1991). *The power is within you.* Carlsbad, CA: Hay House.

Hay, L. (1984). *You can heal your life.* Carlsbad, CA: Hay House.

Heisenburg, W. (1958). *Physics and philosophy.* New York: Harper Torchbooks.

Hicks, E. & Hicks, J. (2004). *Ask and it is given: Learning to manifest your desires*. Carlsbad, CA: Hay House.

Houston, J. (2003). *New time, new mind*. Berkeley, CA: The Prophets Conference. Florida Keys: Conference Recording Service Inc. www.conferencerecording.com

Kaku, M. (1998). *Visions: How science will revolutionize the 21st century*. New York: Anchor Books.

Kitei, L. D. (2000). *The phoenix lights*. Charlottesville, VA: Hampton Roads Publishing.

Kalmansohn, D. (2006, February). *Crystal clear*. Natural Health, 36(2), 14.

Mack, J. (2002). *The limits of scientific materialism*. Lecture presented at the Florida Prophets Conference.

Mack, J. (1994). *Abduction: Human encounters with aliens*. New York: Macmillan.

Marx-Hubbard, B. (2002). *The planetary awakening: How our generation can transform the world*. Berkeley, CA: Conference Recording Service Inc. www.conferencerecording.com

McNiff, S. (1992). *Art as medicine: Creating a therapy of the imagination*. Boston & London: Shambala Press.

McNiff, S. (1994). *Images as angels*. Art Therapy: Journal of the American Art Therapy Association, Vol. 11, No. 1.

McTaggart, L. (2001). *The field: The quest for the secret force of the universe*. London: HarperCollins Publishers.

Mehra, J. (ed.). (1973). *The physicist's conception of nature*. Dordrecht, Holland: D. Reidel.

Moustakas, C. (1990). *Heuristic research: Design, methodology, and application*. Thousand Oaks, CA: Sage.

Pert, C. (2000). *Your body is your subconscious mind*. Colorado: Sounds True.

Pert, C. (1997). *Molecules of emotion: The science behind mind-body medicine.* New York: Scribner.

Postrel, V. (2003). *The substance of style: How the rise of aesthetic value is remaking commerce, culture & consciousness.* New York: HarperCollins.

Ramtha. (2003). *Cracking the code to the extraordinary.* Yelm, WA: Ramtha's School of Enlightenment.

Ramtha. (2005). *Create your day: An invitation to open your mind.* Yelm, WA: Ramtha's School of Enlightenment.

Schucman, H., & Thetford, W. (1992). *A course in miracles.* Mill Valley, CA: Foundation for Inner Peace.

Shakespeare, W. (1997). *As you like it.* New York: Washington Square Press.

Sheldrake, R. (1995). *A new science of life: The hypothesis of morphic resonance.* Rochester, VT: Park Street Press.

Sophia Loren Official Website. (2006). *About Sophia.* Retrieved October 15, 2006, from http://www.sophialoren.com

Telesco, P., & Hall, R. (2002). *Animal spirit: Spells, sorcery and symbols from the wild.* Franklin Lakes, NJ: New Page Books.

Thomson, M. (1989). *On art and therapy: An exploration.* London: Virago.

Tiller, W. A., Dibble, W. E., & Kohane, M. J. (2001) *Conscious acts of creation: The emergence of a new physics.* Walnut Creek, CA: Pavior.

Tiller, W. A. (1997). *Science and human transformation: Subtle energies, intentionality and consciousness.* Walnut Creek, CA: Pavior.

Tolle, E. (1997). *The power of now: A guide to spiritual enlightenment.* Vancouver, Canada: Namaste Publishing.

Van Manen, M. (1990). *Researching lived experience: Human science for an action sensitive pedagogy.* Albany: State University of New York Press.

Vincente, M., Chasse, B., & Arntz, W. (Producers). (2006). *What the bleep!?: Down the rabbit hole* [Movie]. California: Twentieth Century Fox Film Corporation.

Virtue, D. (2005, February). *The romance angels* [audio-cassettes]. Carlsbad, CA: Hay House.

Wesselman, H. (2003). *The journey to the sacred garden: A guide to traveling in the spiritual realms.* Carlsbad, CA: Hay House.

Wesselman, H. (2001). *Vision seeker: Shared wisdom from the place of refuge.* Carlsbad, CA: Hay House.

Wesselman, H. (1998). *Medicinemaker: Mystic encounters on the shaman's path.* New York: Bantam Books.

Wesselman, H. (1995). *Spiritwalker: Messages from the future.* New York: Bantam Books.

Wise, N. (2002). *A big new free happy unusual life.* New York: Broadway Books.

Wolf, F. A. (1999). *The spiritual universe: One physicist's vision of spirit, soul, matter, and self.* Portsmouth, NH: Moment Point Press.

Wolf, F. (1981). *Taking the quantum leap: The new physics for non-scientists.* New York: Harper & Row.

Wyman, M. (2004). *The defiant imagination: An impassioned plea to keep culture at the heart of the Canadian experiment.* Vancouver, Canada: Douglas & McIntyre.

Zukov, G. (1980). *The dancing Wu Li masters: An overview of the new physics.* New York: Bantam New Age Books.

Index

A

ability to surrender 139
acting 30, 50, 151
actors 47, 66, 75, 77, 78, 79, 82, 95, 96, 97, 100, 102, 107, 108, 127, 128, 130, 131, 152
aesthetics 26, 74, 101, 104, 105, 129, 148, 149, 151
affirmations xxi, 8, 16, 17, 18, 48, 59, 72, 111, 112, 119, 122
agent of change xix, 125
agent of inspiration xix, xxi, 125, 134, 141
Air Love xx, 9
aliens 124, 159
Andrews, Julie 18, 111
angels 16, 40, 142, 160, 162, 174
animals 5, 137, 178, 181, 182, 183
Argentine tango 140
artists 11, 12, 45, 47, 48, 54, 60, 85, 99, 126, 127, 128, 150, 157
Artist's Way, The 10, 15, 20, 48, 143, 145, 165
arts xx, 1, 10, 11, 12, 20, 21, 64, 84, 89, 119, 129, 134, 138
assumption of linearity 122
atmospheres 39
audience 9, 10, 11, 12, 25, 27, 29, 33, 37, 38, 41, 42, 43, 50, 51, 54, 58, 65, 67, 72, 78, 79, 83, 84, 112, 127, 128, 129, 134, 138
awareness xix, 1, 2, 3, 6, 7, 8, 10, 13, 18, 20, 54, 64, 104, 114, 121, 123, 125, 126, 133, 135, 169, 180, 181, 183

B

Balm in Gilead 20, 66, 67, 68, 74, 84, 90, 130, 131, 158
beauty 23, 25, 26, 32, 52, 53, 54, 104, 105, 106, 112, 120, 148, 149, 151, 154, 155, 157, 182
bedtime stories 135
Billie 20, 66, 68, 69, 70, 71, 73, 74, 75, 76, 77, 78, 79, 80, 81, 82, 83, 84, 130, 131, 132, 158
Braden, Greg 163
butterflies 26, 155, 177

C

D

E

J

K

L

M

R

S

T

transcendent 11
transformation xix, xxi, 17, 21, 65, 92, 103, 104
transformation of consciousness 12, 22, 113

U

UFO 5, 9, 166

V

vertigo 84, 86, 87, 89, 99
vibrational being 124
vibrational frequency 2, 124, 125
vibrational Universe 124
vision xix, xx, 10, 11, 12, 15, 39, 84, 85, 161, 164, 165
visual imagery 18
visualizations 119, 125

W

What the Bleep Do We Know!? 4, 9, 16, 60, 88, 163, 167, 168